THE OBJECTIVE SELECTION
OF SUPERVISORS

Major Recent Industrial Research Unit Studies

The Wharton School's Industrial Research Unit has been noted for its "relevant research" since its founding in 1921. The IRU is now the largest academic publisher of manpower and collective bargaining studies. Publications include the Major Industrial Research Unit Studies, listed below, and monographs in special series, such as the Labor Relations and Public Policy Series, Manpower and Human Resources Studies, and Multinational Industrial Relations Series.

No. 50 Herbert R. Northrup et al., *Negro Employment in Land and Air Transport: A Study of Racial Policies in the Railroad, Airline, Trucking, and Urban Transit Industries*, Studies of Negro Employment, Vol. V (1971) $13.50.

No. 51 Gordon F. Bloom, Charles R. Perry, and F. Marion Fletcher, *Negro Employment in Retail Trade: A Study of Racial Policies in the Department Store, Drugstore, and Supermarket Industries*, Studies of Negro Employment, Vol. VI (1972).*

No. 53 Charles R. Perry, Bernard E. Anderson, Richard L. Rowan, Herbert R. Northrup, *The Impact of Government Manpower Programs*, Manpower and Human Resources Studies, No. 4 (1975) $18.50.

No. 54 Herbert R. Northrup and Howard G. Foster, *Open Shop Construction* (1975) $15.00.

No. 55 Stephen A. Schneider, *The Availability of Minorities and Women for Professional and Managerial Positions, 1970–1985*, Manpower and Human Resources Studies, No. 7 (1977) $25.00.

No. 56 Herbert R. Northrup, Ronald M. Cowin, Lawrence G. Vanden Plas, et al., *The Objective Selection of Supervisors*, Manpower and Human Resources Studies, No. 8 (1978) $25.00.

No. 57 Herbert R. Northrup et al., *Black and Other Minority Participation in the All-Volunteer Navy and Marine Corps*, Studies of Negro Employment, Vol. VIII (1979).*

No. 58 Herbert R. Northrup and Richard L. Rowan, *Multinational Collective Bargaining Attempts: The Record, the Cases, and the Prospects*, Multinational Industrial Relations Series, No. 6 (1979) $27.50.

Order from the Industrial Research Unit
The Wharton School, University of Pennsylvania
Philadelphia, Pennsylvania 19104

*Order these books from University Microfilms, Inc. Attn: Books Editorial Department, 300 North Zeeb Road, Ann Arbor, Michigan 48106.

MANPOWER AND HUMAN RESOURCES STUDIES

NO. 8

THE OBJECTIVE SELECTION OF SUPERVISORS

A Study of Informal Industry Practices and Two Models for Improved Supervisor Selection

by

HERBERT R. NORTHRUP   RONALD M. COWIN
LAWRENCE G. VANDEN PLAS   WILLIAM E. FULMER

and

ROBERT E. BOLICK, JR.   JANICE R. BELLACE
ANN H. ROSENZWEIG

INDUSTRIAL RESEARCH UNIT
The Wharton School, Vance Hall/CS
University of Pennsylvania
Philadelphia, Pennsylvania 19104
U.S.A.

This study was prepared under two grants from the U.S. Department of Labor, Employment and Training Administration, Nos. 92-42-72-26 and 21-42-75-01. Since grantees preparing research under government sponsorship are encouraged to express their own judgments freely, this study does not necessarily represent the Employment and Training Administration's official opinion or policy. Moreover, the authors are fully responsible for the accuracy of all material developed in the study.

SECOND PRINTING—1981

Foreword

The first-line supervisor or foreman stands between the rank and file and management, his rights often ill-defined, duties ambiguous, and rewards sometimes neglected. Up from the ranks, a part of management, but regularly an orphan from both, the foreman is nonetheless a key cog in the management of personnel and the operation of plants and offices. This is clearly recognized in the literature and has been discussed in meetings of personnel management associations from the beginning of their existence.

The literature on the *selection* of supervisors is, however, rather sparse. Apparently, consideration of how foremen are selected or of why some persons, rather than others, achieve promotion to supervisory posts has not attracted many students of the field. This book is designed not only to lessen this gap but also to suggest ways of improving such selection by substituting more formal methods for the informal mechanisms which appear to be current.

The Objective Selection of Supervisors is the result of two studies, each sponsored by the Employment and Training Administration (formerly the Manpower Administration), United States Department of Labor. These studies were designed to determine what obstacles are in the path of upgrading the disadvantaged and whether it could be demonstrated that the disadvantaged could achieve supervisory positions if objective upgrading systems were utilized. In each case, the results of the studies, although pertinent to the objective, had much wider implications. The first study, made pursuant to Grant No. 92-42-72-26, involved a detailed field investigation of existing supervisor selection procedures. The methodology involved is thoroughly explained and the results are discussed in Part I of this book.

The second study, made pursuant to Grant No. 21-42-75-01, examined and appraised two systems of supervisor upgrading that attempted to select foremen in a more objective manner than is apparently typical. Part II covers this subject. Part III of the book examines the implications of our findings, including the legal implications, pursuant to the Civil Rights Act of 1964 as amended, of failing to utilize objective systems in selecting supervisors.

The Objective Selection of Supervisors (No. 56 of the Major Industrial Research Unit Studies) is published in the Manpower and Human Resources Studies series. This series was inaugurated as part of the Industrial Research Unit's commitment to support the type of research which dates back to the forming of the Unit in 1921 and which was continued in later years in the thirty-one monographs of the Racial Policies of American Industry Series and the eight volumes of the Studies of Negro Employment. Recent studies and monographs published in this series include: *Educating the Employed Disadvantaged for Upgrading,* by Richard L. Rowan and Herbert R. Northrup (1972); *Manpower in Homebuilding,* by Howard G. Foster (1974); the encyclopedic analysis of government manpower activity, *The Impact of Government Manpower Programs,* by Charles R. Perry, Bernard E. Anderson, Richard L. Rowan, and Herbert R. Northrup (1975); *Manpower and Merger,* by Steven S. Plice (1976); and *The Availability of Minorities and Women for Professional and Managerial Positions, 1970-1985,* by Stephen A. Schneider (1977).

This book, which has been developed under my personal direction since its beginning in 1972, is the product of many hands. While serving as a Senior Research Specialist at the Industrial Research Unit, Mr. Ronald M. Cowin developed the research methodology to examine existing selection procedures. After he resigned to accept a position with Honeywell, Inc., the research and writing was led by Mr. William E. Fulmer, assisted by Mr. Robert G. Liney, who did both the statistical and computer work and some interviewing, and also by Mrs. Linda W. Cook and Mr. Kenneth C. Gaus. The draft of Mr. Fulmer's results was accepted as his doctoral dissertation. That manuscript was then thoroughly revised by Ms. Ann H. Rosenzweig, then a graduate student, and myself for the report for Grant No. 92-42-72-26, and submitted to the Employment and Training Administration, U.S. Department of Labor.

A second staff was created for the study of the objective upgrading systems. Mr. Cowin, now with Honeywell, Inc., worked closely with myself and the Honeywell system's creator, Mr. Lawrence G. Vanden Plas, and Professor Richard L. Rowan, who helped to coordinate the work. Mr. Roger M. Fradin, then a graduate student, surveyed the literature on center programs, and Mr. Adolfo Castilla, then also a graduate student, handled the statistics and computer applications. Mr. Robert E. Bolick, Jr., Senior Editor of the Industrial Research Unit's publications,

Mr. Cowin, and I revised and integrated the manuscripts for publication. Ms. Janice R. Bellace, Lecturer in Legal Studies at the Wharton School and Senior Research Specialist—Legal— the Industrial Research Unit, drafted the legal implications section in the concluding part of the book.

Many others assisted in the book's development. The staff of the Office of Research and Development, Employment and Training Administration, especially its Director, Howard Rosen, was continually helpful. Mr. Charles E. Brown, Vice-President, Honeywell, Inc., Dr. H. Weston Clark, Jr., Vice-President of American Telephone & Telegraph Company, and Mr. David Hoyle, Assessment Center Manager for AT&T, provided the necessary clearances and assured the cooperation of their companies in the research. The same was done by executives of the eight companies whose supervisor selection procedures were analyzed, but who must remain anonymous. Messrs. Cowin and Vanden Plas, who served as Honeywell Corporate Project Directors, were assisted by Messrs. A. B. Chudyk, T. R. Ingman, R. O. Mayer, J. N. Newstrom, J. P. Rowles, and P. J. Simpkins, all Honeywell Division Project Managers. Messrs. Cowin and Vanden Plas also authored much of the Honeywell project. Mr. Bolick, assisted by Ms. Donna Fex, did the editing and made up the index. Ms. Frances Rozinski, Mrs. Jenny Spancake, and Ms. Mary M. Booker typed the manuscript, and Mrs. Margaret E. Doyle, our Office Manager, handled the administrative matters associated with the work.

The costs of preparing the study for publication and some of the printing costs were provided by unrestricted grants from the Mobil Oil Corporation, Hercules, Inc., the Weyerhauser Company, and the Rollin M. Gerstacker Foundation, plus additional unrestricted funds from the eighty companies which constitute the Industrial Research Unit's Research Advisory Group. The views expressed and the conclusions reached are my final responsibility and should not necessarily be attributed to the federal government, other grantors, nor to the University of Pennsylvania.

HERBERT R. NORTHRUP, *Director*
Industrial Research Unit
University of Pennsylvania

Philadelphia
August 1978

List of Authors

Herbert R. Northrup, Professor of Industry, Director, Industrial Research Unit and Chairman, Labor Relations Council, The Wharton School, University of Pennsylvania.

Ronald M. Cowin, M.B.A., The Wharton School; Personnel Staff, Honeywell, Inc.; formerly Senior Research Specialist, Industrial Research Unit, University of Pennsylvania.

Lawrence G. Vanden Plas, Personnel Research Administrator, Honeywell, Inc.; developer of the Honeywell Method described herein.

William E. Fulmer, Ph.D., University of Pennsylvania; Professor of Management, University of Alabama; formerly Research Assistant, Industrial Research Unit, University of Pennsylvania.

Janice R. Bellace, J.D., University of Pennsylvania; member of the Pennsylvania Bar; M.S. (Industrial Relations), London School of Economics and Political Science; Lecturer, Legal Studies, The Wharton School; and Senior Research Specialist, Legal, Industrial Research Unit, University of Pennsylvania.

Robert E. Bolick, Jr., M.A., University of Pennsylvania; Senior Editor, Industrial Research Unit, University of Pennsylvania.

Ann H. Rosenzweig, M.B.A., The Wharton School; formerly Research Assistant, Industrial Research Unit, University of Pennsylvania.

TABLE OF CONTENTS

PART TWO

OBJECTIVE SELECTION

PART THREE

CONCLUDING COMMENTS

LIST OF TABLES

LIST OF FIGURES

PART ONE

Upgrading and Selecting Supervisors
Informal Practices

CHAPTER I

Supervisor Selection Study— Background and Methodology

A "supervisor is a person who has been assigned the leader-ship task to assist the organization's higher level managers in moving the organization toward its goals. More specifically, the supervisor is a person who directs or oversees the work of other persons."[1] A "good" supervisor is one who "generates job satisfaction, reduces absenteeism and turnover, improves the quality of work by training his employees, and serves as a source of stability during emergencies."[2]

Thus, supervisors hold a vital and unique position in American business. They are part of the "management team," but also the "connecting link" between management and nonmanagement employees. As illustrated in Figure I-1, supervisors are at the bottom of one work group (management) and, at the same time, only one step removed from the top of another (non-management). Most supervisors obtain their management position by first moving upward through the nonmanagement struc-ture. Being "vital," "one step removed," and the "tie that binds," supervisors have special significance insofar as their selection and upgrading are concerned. Moreover, there are a number of factors which are making the supervisor's job more difficult and, thus, are enhancing the need for effective upgrad-ing and selection methods.

The first-line supervisor, or foreman, is not only responsible for producing the product at approved levels of quality as well as cost, but he is directly responsible for the men and machines under him. As industries continue to expand, and problems

---

[1] A. B. Carroll and T. F. Anthony, "An Overview of the Supervisor's Job," *Personnel Journal*, Vol. 55 (May 1976), p. 229.

[2] Milton M. Mandell, *The Selection Process: Choosing the Right Man for the Job* (New York: American Management Association, Inc., 1964), p. 441.

FIGURE I-1
The Supervisor's Position

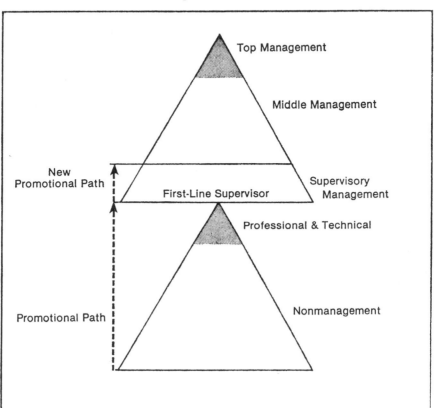

Note: Adapted from C. A. Benson, "New Supervisions: From the Top of the Heap to the Bottom of the Heap," *Personnel Journal,* Vol. 55 (April 1976), p. 178.

of communication arise, the human responsibility becomes increasingly important. The responsibility becomes particularly important in large organizations where the foreman is generally the only member of management who has daily contact with the hourly paid worker.[3]

The increasing importance of the foreman's job is indicated by a mid-1960 survey of plant managers and manufacturing industry vice-presidents. Eighty-seven percent felt that the fore-

[3] M. J. Balma, J. C. Maloney, and C. H. Lawshe, "The Role of the Foreman in Modern Industry," *Personnel Psychology,* Vol. 11 (Summer 1958), p. 196.

man's job carried more responsibility than five years ago. Seven percent said the responsibility was about the same, and only 6 percent felt that the job carried less responsibility.[4]

In light of the importance of the position, it is not surprising that a good foreman has been described as "any company's least expensive and most beneficial fringe benefit" because he "generates job satisfaction, reduces absenteeism and turnover, improves the quality of work by training his employees, and serves as a source of stability during emergencies." [5] Recognizing this, Lawrence A. Appley, former president of the American Management Association, has observed:

> The most vital spot in management is the point of contact between worker and boss. The focal point, the point of greatest return, is the relationship that exists between supervisor and supervised. . . .
>
> More attention should be paid to making this relationship constructive and productive at all levels, than to any other activity.[6]

PRESSURES AFFECTING THE FIRST-LINE SUPERVISOR

The foreman's job has been described as "the most prone to conflicting pressures" of "all industrial roles." [7] If the pressures of the job were at a constant level, the job would be difficult enough, but they seem to be gradually increasing. As Figure I-2 depicts, since 1910 more and more sources of pressure have exerted themselves on industry's first-line supervisor and have made the job increasingly difficult.

Job Pressures

There always have been the dual pressures of maximizing production and minimizing costs. When these goals are not met, the foreman is in the position to receive the brunt of criticism. Higher management can place the blame on lower officials, but by the time the blame has reached the foreman, there is little that he can do but bear it.

---

[4] Bradford B. Boyd and Burt K. Scanlan, "Developing Tomorrow's Foreman," *Training Directors Journal*, Vol. 19 (May 1965), pp. 44-45.

[5] Mandell, *The Selection Process*, p. 441.

[6] George D. Halsey, *Selecting and Developing First-Line Supervisors* (New York: Harper & Brothers, 1955), pp. 1-2, quoting from *Management News*, March 1953.

[7] Kevin Hawkins and Chris Molander, "Supervisors Out in the Cold," *Personnel Management*, Vol. 3 (April 1971), p. 39.

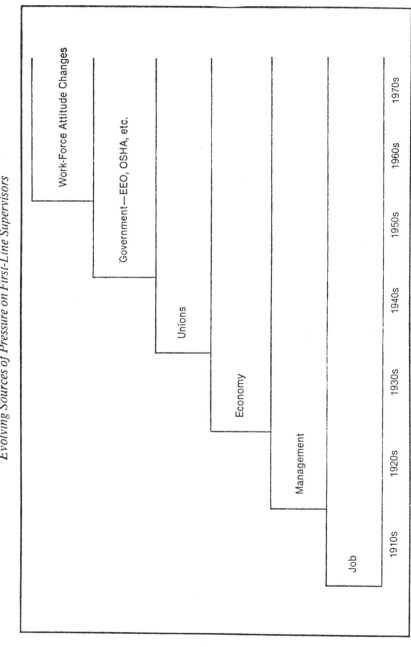

FIGURE 1-2
Evolving Sources of Pressure on First-Line Supervisors

An additional pressure associated with the job of the first-line supervisor is a personal one that stems from making the transition from an hourly employee to a supervisor. Not only does the move give the worker additional responsibilities and perhaps more money, but it may also give him less job security. The foreman is no longer protected by the power of the union and often loses the security of seniority. Whereas he once was paid at least time and one-half for all overtime worked, now he may work more overtime, but receive no extra compensation for it. Whereas he once could utilize the grievance machinery in his own behalf, he now not only is generally denied access to it for his own needs but frequently becomes a stage in the grievance process itself. Finally, whereas he was once "one of the boys" and perhaps even a union official, he now represents management and supposedly develops a new reference group and perhaps a new social group.

Management Pressures

By the 1920s, the days of the omnipotent foremen were beginning to disappear. No longer was the foreman in many companies allowed to operate under loose production schedules and to have "considerable latitude in setting the rates of pay at which he hired men and in making changes in both day rates and piece rates." He also had begun to lose his even greater authority over "hiring, promotion, demotion, discharge, discipline," transfers, overtime and time off.[8]

With the rise of scientific management and other efforts to improve management, many plants divided manufacturing operations into specialized departments. In addition, controls and standards began to be established by management that further restricted the authority of the foreman. Thus, "the foreman found himself surrounded . . . by specialists who were taking over parts of what had formerly been his job" to the point that, often, he was left not only with little more to do than administer the plans and programs developed by various plant departments,[9] but with reduced leverage with which to coerce

----

[8] Sumner H. Slichter, Robert D. Calkins, and William H. Spohn, "The Changing Position of Foremen in American Industry," *Advanced Management*, Vol. 10 (December 1945), p. 155.

[9] Thomas H. Patten, Jr., *The Foreman: Forgotten Man of Management* (New York: American Management Association, Inc., 1968), p. 19.

or cajole the employees into helping him meet production and cost goals.

Even today, it is common for first-line supervisors to voice complaints concerning the pressures imposed on them by their own management. Complaints include pressures from various staff specialists and the lack of support in dealing with employees and unions. In addition, there is the problem of lack of training. It is still common in American industry to find foremen whose only preselection preparation for the job was to be told to report to work the next day in a white shirt.

A major complaint of first-line supervisors is the dead-end nature of their jobs. Although in most American manufacturing plants it is common for blue-collar workers to rise to first-line supervision, it is becoming increasingly futile for blue-collar workers to aspire to higher management positions unless they obtain a college degree. Finally, one hears complaints about lack of adequate compensation and about the rank and file's earning more than supervisors, particularly when the former are paid substantial amounts in overtime earnings.

Economy Pressures

Like most Americans, supervisors have been pressured by the vicissitudes of the economy. In the great Depression of the 1930s, many supervisors lost their jobs. During World War II, others, fearful that the end of the war would mean a return of the depressed situation of the previous decade, sought protection through unionization.[10] Section 2(3) of the 1947 amendments to the National Labor Relations (Taft-Hartley) Act removed government protection of the supervisor's right to unionize,[11] but the short-lived union movement alerted higher

---

[10] See Herbert R. Northrup, "The Foreman's Association of America," *Harvard Business Review*, Vol. 23 (Winter 1945), pp. 187-202.

[11] Section 2(3) of the Taft-Hartley Act states, "the term 'employee' shall . . . not include . . . any individual employed as supervisor. . . ." Section 2(11) defines the term "supervisor" to mean: "any individual having authority, in the interest of the employer, to hire, transfer, suspend, lay off, recall, promote, discharge, assign, reward, or discipline other employees, or responsibly to direct them, or to adjust their grievances, or effectively to recommend such action, if in connection with the foregoing the exercise of such authority is not of a merely routine or clerical nature, but requires the use of independent judgment." For an analysis of how the National Labor Relations Board and the courts administer and interpret this provision, see John E. Abodeely, *The NLRB and the Appropriate Bargaining Unit*, Labor Relations and Public Policy Series, Report No. 3 (Philadelphia: Industrial Research Unit, The Wharton School, University of Pennsylvania, 1971), pp. 204-11.

management to the problems of foremen. Undoubtedly, the result was a greater concern with and more attention to those problems.

More recently, inflation has added both pressure and aggravation to the supervisor's lot—as it has to most of the population. Where the rank and file receive cost-of-living wage adjustments and the supervisors receive merit increases, wage differentials between the two have often narrowed. As noted, with penalty overtime pay paid to the rank and file, differentials may even be reversed. It is asking a lot to expect supervision to remain loyal members of the "management team" under such circumstances. The *Wall Street Journal* reported in early 1978:

> A third of Burlington Northern Inc.'s supervisors return eventually to wage-earner status. That's a big increase over previous levels. . . . A group of New York City engineering supervisors seeks "demotion" to lower job titles. These and similar developments elsewhere are attributed to a desire to make money through overtime.

> Hercules Inc. . . . says its foremen dropped hints about joining unions until the company guaranteed them at least 5% more than total wages, including overtime, of their highest-paid subordinates. Other firms simply authorize overtime for foremen, while United Airlines conducts a personnel survey designed to spot workers willing to forego short-term wage losses because of long-range career goals.[12]

Union Pressures

With the development of organized labor on an industrial basis, collective bargaining demanded new specialization of functions and the attention of higher management in making employee relations decisions. Since unfair labor practices could now be charged against the company because of the action of a supervisor, the foreman in many companies was no longer given broad labor relations authority. Moreover, unions, as management-control devices, have sought to limit foremen's discretion in all aspects of personnel direction. In addition, supervisor's decisions regarding employees can become the object of union grievances. This has increased the conflicting demands from management on supervision. First, there is the demand that the foreman meet production goals. To do so, he may feel it

---

[12] "Labor Letter," *Wall Street Journal*, March 21, 1978, p. 1.

necessary to let employee infractions slip by to insure the cooperation of the union in meeting goals. In addition, he often
is directed to keep grievances at a minimum since they are
costly in money and time. On the other hand, he is frequently
faced with the demand to "run a tight operation" and not "give
the operation away." To accomplish this objective, he may
have to take many disciplinary actions against which the union
will lodge grievances. Moreover, even when in the right, the
foreman may become the victim of harassing grievances as a
union steward or committeeman attempts to limit supervisory
authority even further.

The Government

Although the job of the first-line supervisor has been in-
directly affected by government action for several decades, it
was in the 1960s and 1970s that, through two laws and an
executive order, the government was to have the greatest direct
impact.

With the passage of Title VII of the Civil Rights Act of
1964 and subsequent formation of the Equal Employment Opportunity Commission, and with the issuance of Executive Order 11246 and subsequent formation of the Office of Federal
Contract Compliance Programs, a major emphasis was placed
on having American industry employ minorities and females.
To make the transition to integration easier for all concerned,
a considerable amount of attention has been focused on training
first-line supervisors in the area of human relations. Also affecting the first-line supervisor has been the emphasis on "affirmative action." Under this policy, the pressure on foremen is to
give at least equal (and in some cases preferential) treatment
to minorities in matters of promotion and upgrading, often in
situations where supervision feels others may have greater
qualifications. Thus, the foreman is in the position of trying to
reconcile pressures from the union, the corporation, and the
government, not to mention his own personal feelings.

In 1970, the Occupational Safety and Health Act was passed,
further increasing the responsibilities of the foreman. Under
this law, he is required to find time to give greater emphasis
to safety practices. Not only must he set an example by his
own conduct, but he must train and police his employees in
the matter of plant and personal safety. In addition to these
responsibilities, the act provides another mechanism whereby

irresponsible union leadership or employees can further harass the foreman.

New Work-Force Pressures

By 1970, much attention was being paid to the "new work force." Note was being taken of the better educated work force and of their backgrounds of economic security. Such factors were thought to contribute to worker alienation. This alleged alienation was believed to be evidenced by increasing absenteeism, rejection of overtime, lack of respect for authority, and demands for eliminating dehumanizing working conditions. It remains to be seen what the culmination of such alleged alienation will be. Nevertheless, it is obvious that this situation represents another source of pressure with which the first-line supervisor must deal. Certainly the supervisor's job will not become either easier or subject to less pressures.

EMPIRICAL STUDY OF SUPERVISOR SELECTION

Although few jobs have received as much attention as has the job of first-line supervisor, a search discloses that, at least until recently, the literature on supervisor selection has been relatively sparse. To be sure, scholars have long recognized the importance of supervisor selection, and the literature reflects this fact. Most writings, however, deal with three areas: the role of supervisors, their qualifications, or their training. Some of the literature, of course, concerns itself with supervisor selection, but even that deals largely with different techniques that have been advocated for improving the selection process.

It was for this reason that the Industrial Research Unit devised an empirical study to determine just how supervisors are selected in practice, and applied for and received support from the U.S. Department of Labor, Employment and Training Administration, in carrying it out. It was felt that such a study would be significant as a means not only of learning more about the upward mobility patterns of blue-collar workers but also of providing information about the potential of minorities and women to move upward to supervisory jobs. The study took over two years and focused on the process by which people are selected for first-line supervisory positions. Formal and informal selection practices were studied, and numerous factors that influence selection decisions were investigated and analyzed. Particular attention was given to the personal characteristics of the employees involved to determine why some people benefit from the selection system and others do not.

The study, which is summarized in the following four chapters,[13] deals with three basic questions: (1) What are the common procedures by which hourly employees are upgraded into supervison? (2) What extenuating circumstances, environmental and institutional factors, affect the operation of the upgrading procedures? and (3) What are the personal characteristics of the employees who tend to be upgraded into supervision, and how do they differ from those of employees who are not upgraded? By attempting to isolate the personal, institutional, and environmental factors that affect the selection system, the researchers sought answers to these upgrading processes. (See Table I-1 for definitions of terms.)

Answers to the three questions were pursued by examining in detail the situation in eight manufacturing plants, each chosen from a different industry—paper manufacturing, petroleum refining, electrical manufacturing, chemical manufacturing, food processing, automobile assembly, aircraft manufacturing, and nonferrous metals smelting. The sample represents both a wide range of production processes which would necessitate very different upgrading practices and a variety of employee representation which would also affect promotion procedures. Within the different industries, the particular plants chosen for study reflect different environmental, personal, and institutional factors. Locations vary from small towns to thriving urban centers, and all regions of the country are included. The plants manifest cultural and racial differences as well as disparate economic conditions. Size, skill level, and the extent of government contracting also vary.

Within each plant investigated, attention was restricted to entry level through first-line supervisory positions—those jobs traditionally filled by blue-collar production employees. Interviews were conducted at each plant with various members of line management, including first-line supervisors as well as var-

---

[13] A more complete write-up of each plant studied is found in William E. Fulmer, "Becoming a Supervisor: A Study of Personal Characteristics and Other Factors That Impact on the Process of Upgrading Workers to Supervision" (Ph.D. diss., University of Pennsylvania, 1974).

TABLE I-1
Key Definitions

Internal Labor Market

"An administrative unit, such as a manufacturing plant, within which the pricing and allocation of labor is governed by a set of administrative rules and procedures. The internal labor market, governed by administrative rules, is to be distinguished from the external labor market of conventional economic theory where pricing, allocating, and training decisions are controlled directly by economic variables."[a]

Upgrading

The formal and/or informal processes facilitating the advancement of employees to a higher grade or classification within the internal labor market. Upgrading encompasses the administrative rules or procedures governing training and promotion within an internal labor market as well as any other policies, procedures, or practices that may affect the upward movement of employees within the administrative unit.

Mobility

A broad concept referring to the general movement of employees from one job to another. *Upward mobility* simply refers to movement from a lower job to a higher job. For the purpose of this study, all such movement must take place within the plant being studied.

Personal Factors

Those items that can be used to describe the participants of the internal labor market. They consist of objective characteristics such as age, sex, race, educational attainment, and seniority, and subjective characteristics such as dependability, leadership, initiative, and ability to get along with others.

Institutional Factors

Those variables that are primarily under the control of management, unions, and/or employees of the plant. Examples of such factors are technology, employment practices, plant size, and collective bargaining agreements.

Environmental Factors

Those broad items that are generally beyond the control of the internal labor market but affect it. Examples are geographic location, general economic conditions, public policies, and laws.

[a]Peter B. Doeringer and Michael J. Piore, *Internal Labor Markets and Manpower Analysis* (Lexington, Mass.: D. C. Heath & Co., 1971), pp. 1-2.

ious members of the staff. These interviews provided most of the information necessary for answering the questions concerning the procedures used in upgrading and the factors affecting the system. Collecting data from a sampling of personnel records was also undertaken in an effort to isolate personal characteristics which distinguished those upgraded from those not upgraded.

METHODOLOGY AND DEFINITIONS

Data concerning personnel working at each plant included in the study were subjected to careful examination and analysis. Investigators also visited the various facilities to gather first-hand information from the different perspectives of hourly workers, supervisors, and top management about the upgrading of employees. The researchers then quantified the data and interpreted the results of statistical tests performed on it.

Research into the literature on this topic resulted in a tentative decision to collect data from two sources: interviews with direct participants in the upgrading systems at each plant, and samples of plant records. Five member-plants of a particular corporation were chosen to test the feasibility of the above procedures and to work out the problems involved. Thereafter, the investigators uniformly applied the following methodology to each of the eight plants which constituted the final sample.

Interviews

Personal interviews furnished the bulk of the institutional and environmental data and helped identify both personal factors affecting selection and criteria used in screening potential candidates. Because interviews were conducted with all levels of plant staff involved in the selection process, different forms were developed for each of the four levels of stratification.

1. The *Industrial Relations Department Interview* (see Appendix A), normally occupying a full work day, is composed of questions which focus on both general personnel practices and on the industrial relations activities that affect and/or are part of the selection process. The interview in a smaller enterprise was conducted with the personnel manager (or his assistant if the employee relations office was small), and the interview in a larger operation was divided into functional segments and conducted with the official most familiar with the particular function.

2. The *Plant Manager's Interview* (see Appendix B), designed to last from twenty to thirty minutes, covers his objectives for the selection process, the implementation of those objectives, and the degree of his direct participation in the process itself.

3. Depending on their availability, approximately ten to twenty *Department Heads and/or Superintendents* (see Appendix C)

were interviewed at each plant for thirty to forty minutes apiece. These interviews proved a valuable source of information concerning the process's overall effectiveness, the criteria utilized when selecting candidates, and the overall involvement of these people in upgrading.

4. The *First-Line Supervisors' Interview,* conducted with ten to twenty first-line supervisors at each plant, covers issues such as the foremen's perceptions of requirements and functions pertaining to their job: their motivations for becoming supervisors, their general job satisfaction, and their feelings about the overall effectiveness of the selection system (see Appendix D).

In addition to the questions already mentioned, each management level was also requested to state the criteria which it used to select and/or recommend people for first-line supervision. Such questioning facilitated an examination of management's success in communicating the desirable qualifications to workers in the organization.

Gaining access to the appropriate people was the major impediment to conducting interviews. Because of production needs of the plants and possible union objections, even the more enthusiastic major United States corporations were reluctant to allow interviews with hourly employees. The emphasis of interviewing was therefore directed toward the line managers and particularly the first-line supervisors. Here too, however, difficulties arose, and it was not always possible to conduct interviews on a random basis. Nevertheless, there is no evidence that any of the data provided biased the study's results.

Personnel Files

Except for the very large plants where a smaller proportion was used, a 10 to 20 percent random sample of the personnel files of the production work force was inspected. In addition, data were collected on all first-line supervisors; in the very large plants, samples were mostly limited to supervisory files.

A general, adaptable data form was used with facilitated transfer of information onto computer cards. Statistical manipulations of the data helped to isolate and contrast the quantifiable personal characteristics that distinguished first-level supervisors from hourly employees.

Two major problems arose when dealing with this source of information. First, many plants maintained very incomplete personnel files, often storing no information to supplement the original application forms, which were frequently not in use several decades ago. In addition, most plants had experienced at least one change of application form, particularly during transfers of ownership or in recent years when the government began to restrict the type of information one could solicit from applicants. Some plants had policies which called for the destruction of old records of current employees. Despite the shortcomings, there were usually a sufficient number of sources from which one could develop at least a basic work-force profile.

The second problem associated with personnel files was the sensitivity of the material. Some companies, treating personnel records as confidential documents, did not allow outsiders access. This issue was aggravated by unions' complaints concerning the information distribution.

Miscellaneous Sources

Prior to each visit, the literature was thoroughly searched. Also, requests for information were sent to the plants for such materials as labor contracts, organization charts, progression lines, seniority rosters, copies of personnel policies and procedures, and numerous personnel forms, which proved helpful in anticipating what would be encountered at the plant. This procedure also permitted advance planning of interview schedules and selection of personnel files to be samples. Plant tours, another data source, provided a better understanding of the nature of the production processes and furnished valuable insights into related environmental and institutional factors. Researchers were given such tours prior to interviews whenever possible.

Data Analysis

Both descriptive and quantitative analytical methods were employed in the study. The descriptive analysis utilized a model of organizational behavior, whereas the quantifiable analysis used several statistical techniques.

Organizational Analysis. In Part I, a basic model adapted from the work of Anthoy G. Athos and Robert E. Coffey [14] provides a framework for a systematic discussion of the interaction of environmental and institutional factors with the behavior of pro-

---

[14] Anthony G. Athos and Robert E. Coffey, *Behavior in Organizations* (Englewood Cliffs, N.J.: Prentice Hall, 1968), pp. 90-91.

FIGURE I-3
Upgrading: Organizational Model

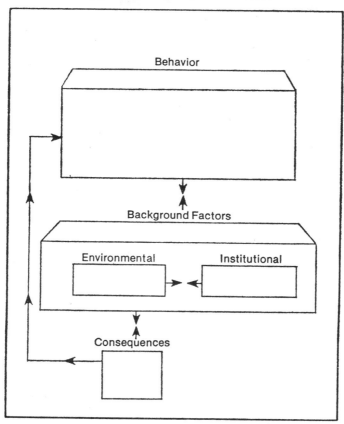

motion systems (see Figure I-3). The procedures themselves of the upgrading systems, their background factors, and the personal characteristics of people that successfully work through the system are also analyzed below.

Statistical Analysis. A major objective of this study, to determine the variables which significantly discriminate between first-line supervisors and hourly employees, was accomplished by the statistical methods of hypothesis testing, discriminant analysis, test of proportions, and criteria clustering. These methods and their use are explained in Table I-2.

TABLE I-2
Explanation of Statistical Methodology

Hypothesis Testing

At the beginning of the section on personal characteristics, tables are presented which list the major quantifiable variables that were available at the particular plant. It was initially assumed that there was no difference between values of quantifiable variables obtained for first-line supervisors and values obtained for hourly employees. This assumption was then tested against the actual values collected from the data and rejected if the data proved otherwise.

Discriminant Analysis

This is a multivariate statistical technique designed to test for interaction between the significant variables. The test served as an index of discrimination to specify how accurately the quantifiable personal data could classify an employee as a first-line supervisor or hourly employee. It also isolated the particular variables which contribute most to this discrimination. A more conservative procedure known as simultaneous confidence intervals was also applied to test for differences between the groups with respect to particular variables.

Test of Proportions

Since a considerable amount of data in personnel files are not truly quantifiable, but are best viewed in terms of proportions (for example, race, sex, and marital status), tests were performed to identify any significant differences in the proportional distribution of these variables between the two groups.

Criteria Clustering

During interviews with plant management, individuals were asked to identify the criteria they used when recommending workers for first-level supervisory positions. A procedure to cluster these criteria was adopted from McQuitty's Elementary Linkage Analysis[a] in the form of a computer program designed to develop groups of closely related variables based on the independent judgments of five people. This technique facilitated ·the assimilation of relatively large numbers of characteristics or criteria identified in the interviews at each plant and the derivation of general criteria that were considered most important in determining who becomes a supervisor. The process was used to list the criteria identified by first-line supervisors and then to list the criteria identified by the higher management, whose judgments usually differed somewhat from those of the former group.

---

[a]Louis L. McQuitty, "Elementary Linkage Analysis for Isolating Orthogonal and Oblique Types and Typal Relevancies," *Educational and Psychological Measurement,* Vol. 17 (1957), pp. 207-29.

CHAPTER II

Supervisor Selection Procedures

The selection of first-line supervisors, or foremen, is a demanding task. The traits required for a good supervisor are not necessarily those of a topflight hourly worker. Thus, the workers from whom the selection is made must often be evaluated on a set of criteria different from those utilized to evaluate them as hourly employees.

Given the significance of the supervisor's job, it was hypothesized that the selection procedures in the plants studied would be carefully thought out and well established. For the most part, however, our study of the procedures in the eight sample plants found little evidence to support this hypothesis.

SELECTION METHODS

Most of the supervisor selection systems studied are decidedly informal. Little written criteria exists upon which to base judgments. Most procedure is highly informal. This, of course, does not mean that the supervisors selected do not satisfy the needs of the companies. Table II-1 summarizes the selection systems used in the eight sample plants.

Smelter, Paper, and Electrical

In the nonferrous smelter, it is the general foreman who makes the major decision within each department on promotion. He recommends a number of candidates to the superintendent, who in turn recommends the foreman's nomination to the plant superintendent. The candidate is then interviewed by top management and is usually approved.

The paper plant follows a similarly informal system. The superintendent confers with his foremen on recommending a candidate, and the choice is almost always approved by the mill manager.

TABLE II-1
First-Line Supervisor Selection

Plant	Formality	Group vs. Independent Decision	Involvement of Top Management	Involvement of Lower Management	Sources of Replacement
Nonferrous Smelter	Very informal; general foreman makes major decision.	Group consultation.	Plant superintendent reviews decisions of supervisor and has choice approved by at least one higher level.	General foreman consults with foremen and recommends candidates to his superintendent.	Most "come up through the ranks."
Paper Manufacturer	Very informal; new system is being implemented.	Group decision.	General superintendent and mill manager review the recommendation.	Handled almost exclusively by line managers; superintendent asks assistants and foremen for opinions and recommendations and refers to upper management.	People from the top of their respective progression lines.
Electrical Products Manufacturer	Informal procedures due to small size of the plant.	Tends to be made by top management; group interview.	Personnel office may recommend; superintendents, general foreman, and personnel interview candidates; superintendent has final say.	General foreman and superintendent decide; most supervisors and foremen are not consulted.	Current employees get first consideration, generally the next level below; plant must frequently recruit from the outside.

Chemical Manufacturer	No formal procedures, but general practices followed.	Group decision among top management.	Plant manager, operations manager, personnel manager, superintendent, and supervisor meet and review candidates; if there is a disagreement, the plant manager makes the final decision.	Superintendents consult supervisors; supervisors do not consult foremen, but recommend candidates after checking files.	Most selected from group-one employees who have some experience due to supervisory responsibilities of a group-one job; only a little departmental line crossing.
Aircraft Manufacturer	Very informal; reflects recent layoffs and downgrading of supervisors.	Manufacturing management and personnel decide together; general foreman has most impact.	Personnel office recommends and confers with line management.	Line management, from assistant foreman to director of manufacturing, recommends; general foreman decides on list.	In the past, leadmen were used; now supervisors are usually grade ones unless previously laid off or downgraded supervisors are available.
Petroleum Refinery	Informal procedures; guidelines not always practiced.	Personnel and line management review decisions; when 2 candidates are equal, seniority is important.	Department head develops list, submits to director, who submits to personnel office; candidates tested, used on a temporary basis; joint committee for permanent opening reviews and recommends; decision depends primarily on top management which reviews all decisions.	Occasionally consulted, but rarely is anyone lower than general foreman involved; first-line supervisors evaluate temporaries; 70% of the selection decision is based on their evaluation.	Try to maintain equal ratio of college to hourly sources in operations maintenance; promote from within; come from top of progression line on probation; if they perform well, they are retained.

TABLE II-1 (continued)

Plant	Formality	Group vs. Independent Decision	Involvement of Top Management	Involvement of Lower Management	Sources of Replacement
Food Processing Plant	Somewhat formal; general procedures followed.	All potentials are identified in yearly reviews; when a position opens, several management levels are involved.	If a college graduate is to be chosen, division manager selects; personnel dept. reviews recommendations for possible problems.	If an hourly is upgraded, lower levels are involved; degree of involvement of first-line supervisors varies between departments.	For production, a utility service operator position is the training ground; maintenance supervisors come from top classification or from inspectors (if department lines are crossed).
Automobile Assembly Plant	Very formal; extensive application form, training program after selection.	Committee of comptroller, EEO coordinator, production manager, personnel director, material supervisor, directors, and top officials interviews applicants.	Plant manager's assistant confers with personnel.	Consultation with foremen and superintendents.	Selected mostly from assemblers—not those with key positions because those are usually the ones with most seniority and not necessarily the best.

Because of the small size of the electrical products plant, its system is also informal. The superintendent, again, consults with the general foreman on candidates within the hourly ranks. The general foreman usually does not involve the first-line supervisor in the selection procedure, but the personnel office may recommend candidates to supplement the list. When the choice is narrowed to a few candidates, the union is notified, and an informal interview is conducted by the superintendent, his general foremen, and a personnel representative. If there is a disagreement about the final choice, the superintendent makes a decision to be approved by the manufacturing manager.

Chemical and Aircraft

The chemical plant's procedure is very similar until the point at which top management becomes involved. Here, instead of conducting an interview, the personnel director prepares a "spread sheet" on all candidates to be used for a top management meeting. The sheet lists data such as date of hire, highest job held, age, education, performance evaluation results, and test scores. If no consensus is reached, the group adjourns so that additional thought may be given the matter. If after a few days, there is still no agreement, the plant manager makes the final decision.

A unique situation controls the aircraft plant's supervisor-upgrading procedures. In the late 1960s, approximately eight hundred first-, second-, and third-level supervisors were either reduced to hourly employees or laid off. When an opening now arises, this discharged pool is informally reviewed, and the assistant foreman and foreman recommend two or three possible candidates. Simultaneously, the internal placement office also develops a potential list, and negotiations between the two groups decide the final selection. Prior to the time of the large layoff, the first source of candidates was the pool of recently laid-off supervisors from nearby company operations; the second, requests; and the third, hourly workers. In some departments, all relevant first- and second-line supervisors may vote on the individuals up for selection. The general foreman reviews the individual files of these people and submits the decision to the superintendent. Some general foremen have developed rating forms to assist them in formalizing the evaluations of lower management officials.

Petroleum and Food

The petroleum refinery uses another informal method. Temporary supervisors are designated to work as supervisors when incumbents are away from work because of sickness, vacations, or absenteeism, or when extra supervisors are needed. Either the director and superintendent or the general foreman (depending on the department) periodically reviews the temporary's potential, as indicated by the evaluation he receives from the first-line supervisors. At this point, the procedure becomes a bit more formalized. Each department head reviews the list of temporaries and selects a few candidates for testing. They are administered a career preference test and a temperament test designed to aid the employee's understanding of his strengths and weaknesses. Although not intended for screening, the test is often employed in such a fashion.

When a permanent opening arises, the appropriate director chooses the best temporary to fill the position. This choice is made either by reviewing foremen's recommendations and arriving at a group decision with general foremen and superintendents or, as sometimes is done, by arriving at a decision without any consultation. The choice is reviewed by the division managers and the refinery manager.

As in the aircraft plant, the refinery's personnel department also selects its best candidate. If there is a discrepancy between its decision and management's choice, a selection committee composed of the director, manager, department head, and two personnel officials reviews the matter. When the two candidates are relatively equal, seniority becomes an important criterion.

The food processing plant prepares in advance for supervisory openings. Each year, the division heads submit to the personnel office a list of all potential supervisors. In addition, when evaluating current first-line supervisors, area managers must designate backstops for each position. They must also identify those employees who will be considered backstops in two years. Developing such lists is frequently done after consulting with lower management, including first-line supervisors. The involvement of first-line supervisors in the actual choice of the replacement varies depending upon the area manager involved.

The area manager carries the major responsibility for recommending backstops and candidates. But, although most area managers feel that the final decision is a group decision reached together with the division manager, the division manager feels that he alone makes the decision. Whichever is the actual case, the decision is reviewed by the plant manager, the assistant plant manager, and the personnel office (the personnel office is informally involved all along, receiving candidates' histories and bringing pertinent facts concerning them to the attention of management).

Automobile Assembly

The only formalized, established selection system in the plants studied is that of the automobile assembly plant. The local officials spent much time developing the procedures and have been relatively successful in convincing all levels of management of the importance of selecting first-line supervisors.

As the need for new foremen arises, notices are posted which encourage workers to apply for the training program. The application requests all pertinent personal data such as age, marital status, dependents, education, past jobs, and military experience. In addition, employees are asked why they wish to become supervisors.

The applications are reviewed by the personnel office, and significant occurrences in the individual's personnel file are noted. The applications are then sent on to the official in the employee's area who is directly under the plant's supervisor. This official consults with the superintendent and general foreman and sometimes interviews the candidate. The application is then returned to the personnel office with appropriate comments and recommendations concerning the employee's promotion.

At the personnel office, the application is reviewed by personnel and line management. The committee attempts to discern why certain applicants are rejected, and what could be done to help them qualify in the future. These employees are encouraged to apply for the next class.

Those individuals who are recommended undergo twenty-minute interviews with the selection committee: two superintendents, the production manager, the personnel director, and the salaried personnel supervisor. The committee questions the applicant about his motivation and qualifications for a supervisory position as well as about his background and interest. The candidate is graded at the end of the interview.

When all applicants are interviewed, the committee selects the top people to fill the open positions. A twelve-week training program ensues. During the first six weeks, the trainees rotate through various line and staff departments to learn the functions of each. During the last six weeks, the trainees work in each section of the department sponsoring them. They are usually assigned a specific foreman group and are often assigned a number of employees for supervision and gradually assume more and more independence.

Also during this twelve-week period, the last hour of each day is spent in classroom training. These sixty hours encompass sessions on such topics as labor relations, the new work force, occupational safety, management aims, fair employment practices, human relations, principles of management, and communications.

During the latter six weeks, each week, the supervisors indicate each trainee's strengths and weaknesses, make recommendations, and state whether they would like to have a particular foreman on permanent assignment. Each evaluation is reviewed by both the production manager and personnel director.

The trainee provides the system with additional feedback by commenting on the overall effectiveness of the program and particular aspects of the training. At the third stage of the process, the trainees are assigned temporary status as foremen for fifteen weeks, which are either continuous or segmented into parts of not less than two weeks each. After evaluation, the trainee enters the fourth phase of the process and is placed on the availability list. When an opening arises, the superintendents and general foremen attempt to select from this list a man who has expressed interest in that particular area. The final selection, as all other decisions in the procedure, is reviewed by the selection committee for approval.

Compared with the other systems studied, this one best achieves its purpose: it carefully screens all potential candidates and, through tests and frequent performance evaluations, selects the best man for the difficult job. There is no informal decision making; all decisions are reviewed and approved with the same criteria used to measure each applicant.

SOURCES OF SUPERVISORS

Conforming to the philosophy of selecting only the best, the automobile plant does not have a tendency to choose first-line supervisors from hourly employees holding key positions. Although several line managers indicated that the utility men and trainers would make excellent training positions for first-line supervisors, these positions are occupied predominantly either by the most senior employee or by an ex-foreman who could not handle the foreman's job. Thus, the employees with the greatest supervisory potential do not necessarily fill the key positions.

Most of the other plants in this study do not follow this seemingly worthwhile practice. In the paper plant, the individuals considered for supervisory positions are those in the top jobs of the respective progression lines. In the pulp mill, for example, training operators are considered "equivalent to assistant foremen" even though they are a part of the bargaining unit.

The smelter candidates also come up through the ranks. Here, however, almost all have spent time as "rerates"[1] prior to promotion. Maintenance rerates almost always come from the craftsman positions and are among the best in the shop, but rerates in operations have no specific origin. Some have as little as six months of service at the plant.

At one time, the aircraft manufacturer used leadmen positions as training ground for supervisors. Since leadmen are part of the bargaining unit, however, and consequently are under union control, the plant now selects supervisors from grade-one employees, who already supervise some lower level workers. To compensate for this very minimal training, some foremen occasionally give added responsibilities to certain employees in order to "bring them along."

The group-one employees of the chemical manufacturer, unlike those at the aircraft plant, receive extensive supervisory experience while on the job. They are responsible for an entire operation and have helpers working for them. These group-one people are also the more senior workers. In the laboratory areas of the chemical plant, simply being a group one is not sufficient justification for being considered for a supervisory position. Because one of the three laboratories involves a faster turnaround in testing and thereby subjects the employee to greater job pressures, there is a tacit understanding that one must work in that laboratory to become a supervisor.

Foreman positions in the food processing plant may be filled either by a college graduate interviewed by the division man-

---

[1] Rerates are hourly employees who have been selected by their supervisors, often in consultation with the general foreman, to work temporarily as foremen when the permanent employee is absent due to sickness, absenteeism, or vacation. Despite their temporary work in supervision, rerates are still members of the hourly work force.

ager or by an inside worker selected after consultation with lower level management. Management is presently attempting to attain a one-to-one ratio of college graduates to hourly employees. If the hourly employee is considered, he usually trains as a utility operator, a position in which ability has traditionally been the predominant criterion. The utility operator is often called the "working" or "assistant" supervisor. He can handle all department jobs, and he trains employees and deals with emergencies.

In the maintenance division, the supervisors usually come from the "A" craftsmen, who work under limited supervision. When departmental lines are crossed in selecting supervisors, inspectors are the most frequent source of candidates. They have extensive visibility during working hours and are likely to be well known by members of management.

The petroleum refinery, adhering to its strict seniority policy, selects the temporary supervisors from the top of the progression lines. If these men perform well, they are retained. If they perform poorly, they may not be given a second chance.

In most of the plants studied, there are fairly well established positions from which most supervisors are selected. Often these positions are occupied by the most senior people. Ability as an operator or craftsman is not necessarily the criterion for candidate selection in the majority of the facilities.

SUPERVISORS' EVALUATION OF SELECTION PROCEDURES

It is not surprising that foremen often voice complaints concerning the informality and unreliability of the selection systems. For example, several foremen at the nonferrous smelter indicated the need for an improved system, and some attemped to implement their own techniques (such as rating forms or written justifications for decisions) to standardize the selection. Similarly, a number of foremen in the paper plant voiced concern over their current selection procedures. It was felt that the lead time in selecting replacements was too long, and that there was no established procedure for selection or for training. As a result, some departments were exploring new methods of selection and training, such as using college graduates or having potential supervisors work with supervisors who were approaching retirement.

The foremen in the food processing plant expressed dissatisfaction with the lack of preselection training for supervisors other than the position of utility man. They felt that potential candidates should be informed of the nature and responsibilities of the job, given advice on self-improvement, and shouldered with some responsibilities for training purposes.

Although most foremen at the petroleum refinery expressed satisfaction with the selection process, some complained about the failure of management to follow the formal selection procedures in all cases. Also, it was felt that all potential candidates should be interviewed, not just those whom the manager wants.

The chemical manufacturer's foremen expressed the belief that it was "important that we know a man wants to be a foreman." Although the higher level supervisors were pleased with the current system, the lower level supervisors, having at one time actively participated in the system, expressed resentment over their current exclusion from the process.

In 1969, the smelter's general corporate division developed a program for selecting and training supervisors to be administered by the industrial relations department. Under the program, the supervisors would regularly review their workers' performances and nominate those who, in their opinion, exhibited the requisite qualities for a successful supervisor. The nomination included completion of a thirteen-question "Supervisory Selection Guidelines," which covers all aspects of the employee under consideration. The formal program did not specify how the final selection was to be made from the list of nominees.

The paper mill managers at the paper manufacturing plant felt that the quality of workers in the top hourly jobs was not sufficiently high for supervisory work. As a result of this and the expected turnover in the near future because of retirements, a new system was implemented. All employees who were "third hands" [2] or higher were rated by all foremen on personality and performance characteristics. The overall score for each individual was compared with factors such as age, seniority, education, and test scores. Of the seven people selected, five were the top people on the overall rating scores, and the other

---

[2] Third hands are third from the top of the paper mill progression line. "Machine tender" is the top position, "back tender" the next, and the remaining jobs are numbered from four to seven.

two employees excelled in educational levels and scores on mechanical aptitude tests and intelligence tests. None of the employees considered, however, had fewer than twenty-one years of seniority. Since all seven employees were only "back tenders" or third hands at the time of selection, it was necessary that they be familiar with the higher jobs in the department. Consequently, a special six-month training program was developed. One-half the time was spent on the job; the other half, in classroom training based on a specially prepared manual.

The petroleum refinery has formally established procedures for upgrading workers, but they have not been followed. The formal system requires each department head to compile a list of employees to be given first consideration for openings. The list of candidates is submitted to the appropriate director and manager, who, in turn, submits the list to the personnel office. The candidates are tested and used on a temporary basis whenever needed for vacation relief or sickness relief. When a permanent opening occurs, a committee of top management considers each candidate according to his performance evaluations as an employee and temporary supervisor. The recommendations of the committee are forwarded to the refinery manager by the area manager who has the opening.

At present, the chemical manufacturing plant is sponsoring a study of the role of the foreman. The intent of the study is to develop a list of major responsibilities of foremen and then to evaluate all current foremen's performance in these areas. It is hoped that the study results can ultimately be used to improve the training of supervisors and perhaps the selection procedures themselves.

CONCLUSIONS

Tests or any other objective criteria for rating potential supervisors are not generally used in the plants studied. Most plants rely on a general consensus of the foreman and top management for selecting the best candidates to fill a position. Sometimes the personnel office becomes involved, and sometimes the candidate must pass through interviews. Almost always, top management must approve the decision, but the approval is usually based upon the superintendent's recommendation.

The candidates that are selected as potential supervisors generally originate from a particular employee classification or position which is considered either good training ground for supervisors or the position which is highest on the progression line (and occupied by the person with the most seniority). Even in the former case, however, the person occupying that key position usually has the most seniority since the upgrading of hourly workers is predominated by a reliance on seniority.

At least five of the plants studied are presently developing more objective or formal procedures for selecting supervisors. Implementing these systems, however, will take a long time. The personnel of the various plants have established set methods and are not eager to uproot their present systems.

CHAPTER III

Factors Affecting Systems for Selecting Supervisors

Besides the structure of the system in which the decision to upgrade is made are a number of other factors influencing the decision. As explained in chapter I, we have grouped these factors under three headings: (1) environmental factors specific to each plant, (2) institutional factors enmeshed within the pertinent upgrading system, and (3) personal factors related to the individual workers. All contribute to the results of the upgrading system. The first two factors are discussed in this chapter; the third, in chapter IV.

ENVIRONMENTAL FACTORS

In developing and researching the monographs and books in the *Racial Policies of American Industry Series* and the *Studies of Negro Employment,* some fourteen hypotheses were tested as determinants of company racial policies.[1] These hypotheses include factors that are herein defined as environmental, such as (1) the demand for labor, (2) the time and nature of the industry's development, (3) the mores of the community, (4) community crises or developments, (5) locational factors, and (6) governmental relationships. It will be seen that these factors are equally important in supervisor selection and upgrading.

---

[1] These hypotheses are set forth in Herbert R. Northrup et al., *Negro Employment in Basic Industry,* Studies of Negro Employment, Vol. I (Philadelphia: Industrial Research Unit, The Wharton School, University of Philadelphia, 1970), pp. 4-10. Each volume in this series and each monograph in the Racial Policies of American Industry Series examine these hypotheses in light of the facts found in the industry or industries studied. (See back pages for lists of these works.)

The Demand For Labor

Periods of prosperity mean increased production and sales and, hence, labor demand. In such times, management is likely to move rapidly to promote persons to supervisory positions, sometimes without paying too much heed even to such degree of objectivity as exists in the upgrading system. As a paper plant assistant superintendent stated, "If business is good, promotions are good."

The paper plant has previously had some negative feedback on its policies. As greater emphasis was placed on production and profitability, the company became less concerned with its employees, and little corporate guidance was given to plants in areas such as upgrading and promotion. Each plant was allowed to follow its own procedures as long as it remained profitable. Some line managers, however, now feel that, since the expansion slowdown in the early 1970s, the corporation has been paying more attention to people and improving upgrading opportunities.

Now the plant force has contracted, and the need for supervisors is reduced. Such developments have had deleterious effects on feelings of job security and plant loyalty. One young worker, a plant employee since high school, has passed through two layoffs in the past ten years and is currently at the bottom of his progression line. Although he is "capable," and his father is a "good" first-line supervisor, he has become a militant union leader. If such layoffs occur often, employees may become less and less willing to accept supervisory positions, regardless of how well thought-out the selection procedure is.

Because the aircraft company relies heavily on government contracts, product demand is determined by presidential actions and congressional appropriations, which fluctuate widely from year to year. The Vietnam buildup and subsequent phasing down of operations created a significant boom-and-bust cycle in the plant. The increase of eighteen thousand employees between 1965 and 1967 opened numerous opportunities for blue-collar workers to be upgraded into supervision. Some blue-collar workers rose from the lowest to the highest position within fourteen months, a phenomenon resulting in a number of relatively young first-line supervisors with little experience who were sometimes selected without due consideration.

Since the drop in product demand in 1967, over fourteen thousand hourly workers have been laid off. As a result, ap-

proximately eight hundred first-, second-, and third-line supervisors have also been either downgraded or laid off. This pool of
downgraded supervisors is the first source of candidates for
promotion. Of course, the massive downgrading enabled the
plant to retain only its best supervisors, a learning situation
beneficial to those employees who will eventually be upgraded
into supervision, but a situation not conducive to good morale
or understanding. Only the best hourly employees were retained,
and the foreman's work was made easier because he now works
with "people who know what they are doing," but, of course,
this applies only to the *retained* foremen.

As to be expected, there has been some bitterness among
the first-line supervisors over the promotion denials and especially the downgrading. One foreman felt that 80 percent
of the former assistant foremen would probably reject the
opportunity to become a supervisor again if recalled. Moreover, some hourly employees are now reluctant to accept promotion into supervision because of the job insecurity. They had
witnessed supervisors being upgraded and downgraded or laid
off on at least two occasions, and they prefer the relative security of hourly jobs.

The automobile industry faces a different set of problems.
Yearly model changes necessitate changes in the assembly lines
and hourly jobs. Besides bearing the responsibility for dealing
with material and labor shortages while meeting production
deadlines, the first-line supervisor also becomes the focus of
employees' complaints and grievances over these annual changes.
In addition, the yearly buildup of five hundred to eight hundred
employees every August tests the supervisor's ability to orient
and train new and often inexperienced employees in the job.
Several plant officials felt that the frustrations and difficulties
associated with a model change discourage many hourly employees from seeking supervisory positions.

The carefully developed evaluations followed in the automobile
assembly plant as part of its upgrading procedure have been
to some extent offset by the volatile nature of employment.
Second shifts have been established and abolished several times
during the last few years, and downgradings and layoffs of
supervisors and, again, some discouragement to those who might
otherwise seek supervisory positions were caused.

The electrical products plant, having experienced a contraction in the work force since the 1940s, faces a different problem.

Layoffs at the time were based on seniority, a procedure which left mostly the older workers employed. As they retired and new employees were hired, a bimodal seniority distribution was created. Although the quality of the workers has not been adversely affected, the older workers occupy the higher level jobs, and promotion to supervision for new hires has been almost impossible.

Of course, even when demand is high, a continuation of low turnover and capital intensity can result in few openings. The petroleum refinery is a good example of this. A recent survey of sixty-seven of the seventy-two first-line supervisors at this plant showed that the average supervisor had been hired as an hourly worker at the age of twenty-three, but was not promoted into supervision until he was forty-six. Although there are indications that many jobs will soon open because of a large number of retirements, seniority will insure much stability in the supervisory force and few openings for young persons or newly employed minorities.

The Time and Nature of Development

The paper plant came South in the 1930s and, following the mores of the community, employed blacks only in manual labor, woodyard work, and certain other jobs. Moreover, blacks were employed under considerably different criteria than whites because blacks were basically nonpromotable. After the passage of the Civil Rights Act of 1964, the company faced EEO requirements that were difficult to meet because most blacks did not have the background or education to qualify for promotion except in the woodyard.[2] Similarly, southern mores formerly proscribed the use of females in mill jobs (although not during World War II). Again, this has amplified EEO problems because neither blacks nor females have had the requisite experience to qualify as supervisors.

When the petroleum refinery was started, the industry simply did not employ minorities as production workers. With hiring

[2] For background in this situation, see "The Negro in the Paper Industry," in Herbert R. Northrup et al., *Negro Employment in Southern Industry*, Studies of Negro Employment, Vol. IV (Philadelphia: Industrial Research Unit, The Wharton School, University of Pennsylvania, 1971); and Richard L. Rowan and Herbert R. Northrup, *Educating the Employed Disadvantaged for Upgrading*, Manpower and Human Resources Studies, No. 2 (Philadelphia: Industrial Research Unit, The Wharton School, University of Pennsylvania, 1972).

at a low ebb for many years, this determined the character of the supervisory force until well after 1964.

Although all these plants have been affected by affirmative action requirements, none has been involved in areas of serious race riots or similar major incidents. The crises of the 1960s, however, pushed all the companies to increase their minority employment, to enhance upgrading programs, and to seek out qualified minorities for supervisory positions.

The electrical plant has for some years been relatively marginal and is expected to close in the near future. Community pressures to keep it open have been strong and probably have added to its life and, thus, to continued opportunities for upgrading.

The severe environmental pressures placed upon the paper, chemical, petroleum, and smelter operations have lessened the opportunities for upgrading. These companies have poured millions into equipment to help them meet water and air standards. The equipment not only reduces pollution but, for the paper and smelter plants, reduces manpower needs and, hence, the need for supervision. The petroleum refinery, however, found that the pollution equipment requires more—not fewer—supervisors, but because of the uncertainties and costs created by the federal government's ambiguous pollution standards and energy policies, it has postponed indefinitely expansions which would create additional supervisory positions.

Most of the environmental pressure comes from the federal and state governments and from outside the plant communities, but particularly in the case of the paper and smelter plants, there are strong community environmental groups whose pressure affects the future of the operations in question. Since the investments in pollution abatement are generally neither demand creating nor job creating—but often, as noted, the opposite—the net effect is to preclude the investment which would create more jobs and further opportunities for upgrading to supervisory positions.

Locational Factors

Also affecting upgrading procedures are both the region or area in which a facility is located and the facility's location within the region or area—center city, suburban, urban, or rural. Thus, if the region or area has a large percentage of an ethnic or racial group, the supervisory force may reflect this fact;

but if the plant is located on the outskirts of a city, and blacks are concentrated on the opposite side of the city, the black ratio in the plant is likely to be much smaller.

Table III-1 compares the percentage of minorities in the sample plants with that in the labor force and supervisory force. Although five of the plants are located in or near metropolitan areas which have sizable minority populations, and two others are found in the South, the percentages of minorities in the work force and supervisory positions are not at all consistent. In all cases but one for which data are available, the minority work force has a greater percentage of the hourly jobs than of supervisory positions. This is undoubtedly attributable to the lower skill, lack of work experience, and educational background of minorities, but location is a problem, too.

For example, the electrical products plant, the exception to this rule, is located in the heart of center city and surrounded by a black neighborhood. It began drawing on this population during the 1960s and has advanced many long-service minority workers to supervisory jobs. On the other hand, the aircraft manufacturer is located far from the concentrations of blacks in its metropolitan area. The highly skilled nature of the work and the educational background required reduce the number of blacks available for supervision. Moreover, a supervisor is on call for emergencies, and the long commute required of many blacks has discouraged them from accepting promotions.

The high percentage of minorities in the smelter's supervisory force is attributable to its location in an area to which Mexican-Americans were attracted and to its upgrading of these workers.

The poor public transportation around the petroleum refinery also discourages minorities who cannot afford cars from seeking employment or upgrading at the plant. Some workers who do own cars, however, have rejected upgrading offers because accepting promotion would require a change in shift that necessitates driving to work during rush hour.

The food processing plant is uniquely located in a rural area where agriculture has been the mainstay of the local economy. Because the more ambitious youth move to the cities to work or to attend college, the plant, the largest employer in the immediate area, has been able to employ the best of the remaining labor market. Until recently, ambitious blacks left the area because of lack of opportunities. Although this is no longer true, the past situation has decreased black availability for supervisory positions.

TABLE III-1
Minority Statistics

Plant	Type of Locale	Labor Market %	Total Plant Work Force %	Total Hourly Work Force %	Plant First-Line Supervisors %
Nonferrous Smelter	Metropolitan	4.0	$7.0^a/3.0^b$	$8.0^a/3.0^b$	$3.0-4.0^a/2.0^b$
Paper Manufacturer	Small city (South)	45.0	23.0	28.0	N.A.
Automobile Assembly Plant	Metropolitan	12.0	N.A.	20.0	5.0
Aircraft Manufacturer	Metropolitan	16.0	10.0	16.0	3.0
Chemical Manufacturer	Small city (North)	14.0	10.0	N.A.	7.0
Food Processing Plant	Rural (South)	17.0	20.0	N.A.	4.1
Electrical Products Manufacturer	Metropolitan	32.0	11.0	13.0	19.0
Petroleum Refinery	Metropolitan	18.1	6.5	8.0	less than 1.0

[a]Mexican-Americans.
[b]Blacks.
N.A. Not available.

There is, moreover, considerable prestige associated with working at the food plant, especially working in a supervisory capacity. Hourly employees are eager to work there and exhibit a relatively low turnover and absentee rate because they are already accustomed to working hard on the farms. The supervisor's job is consequently easier and more desirable than comparable work at other facilities. The major problem confronting management in this plant is the employees' reluctance to work overtime. Some hourly employees moonlight by farming in their off-hours and do not want supervisory jobs which often require extra hours of work. This is often a problem associated with supervisor selection in plants located in rural areas.

The impact of education on the potential for promotion is particularly significant in some areas. Thus, in the paper plant, most of the work force was educated when schools were still segregated, and most blacks attended schools which were inferior to those of the whites. Also, blacks tended to drop out of school earlier than whites. With the increasing complexities of production, education has become more important in the upgrading process, and minority promotions into supervision have been slowed as a result.

The petroleum refinery faces a similar problem because most minority employees have been educated in poor city schools near their homes. To be upgraded at this plant, an employee must pass through rigorous training and testing which necessitates a strong educational background. This automatically excludes a large percentage of the hourly minorities from consideration. We have already noted the similar problem in the aircraft plant.

Conservative religious attitudes and practices often influence the readiness of workers to accept supervisory positions. After his promotion, one worker at the paper manufacturing plant returned to the hourly ranks because he refused to work on Sundays. A similar situation exists in the food processing plant, where some females who may have otherwise worked in the plant refuse to accept jobs because they will not wear the overalls required by the company.

A strong feeling of solidarity among the sect members of the food plant and of different religious groups in the smelter makes adjustment for outsiders difficult not only within the hourly work force but also within the ranks of the supervisors. The food manufacturing plant is located in a town described as having a "well-defined social structure." Because most blacks already living in the area are in a relatively "low class structure," it is particularly difficult to attract black college graduates to fill supervisory positions.

The churches of the employees at both the smelter and the paper plant place heavy emphasis on morality, honesty, and integrity. This is reflected in the supervisors' choices of hourly workers for upgrading. At least one superintendent at the paper facility said that he would consider an individual's moral standards before recommending him for supervision. He was concerned that a supervisor's personal life might have a bad influence on his subordinates.

The religion followed by most workers in the smelter area encourages the women to remain in the home and to leave the work to the men. This same attitude typifies the community which constitutes the labor market for the food processing plant.

There, young people marry early, wives are considered secondary members of the family, and females do not seek work outside the home. This plant has the lowest female percentage of total plant workers of all the plants studied, only 28 percent.

The effects of these attitudes on upgrading are obvious. In the food plant, one line manager specifically said that there has been "no attempt to upgrade them [women]. They may not have the necessary qualifications." The union, also, is resistant to dropping departmental seniority in favor of plant seniority because this would facilitate upgrading for females.

The petroleum refinery experiences another difficulty with upgrading women workers. The plant, located in a heavily industrialized neighborhood, simply cannot attract the female force that the city, providing after-hours and lunch-hour shopping opportunities, can attract. Consequently, few women apply for hourly jobs in the refinery, and even fewer work in supervisory capacities.

Governmental Policies

We have already noted that governmental policies on pollution affect the number of supervisory jobs to which workers can be upgraded. More important is the pressure exerted by the federal government for companies to develop affirmative action plans to give special, or favored, status to minorities and women. Such pressure is especially heavy on government contractors, which include all eight companies studied here, but only six of the actual plants.

In the electrical products plant, management has already been successful in upgrading black employees into supervision by committing itself to "examining minorities presently employed to be certain they are being considered and trained for higher positions." Almost no blacks were hired prior to 1960, but now, according to one foreman, management not only hires blacks but is "under pressure to promote blacks. We were told to 'get the best you can.'" To insure the hiring of minorities, the plant has signed an agreement with the local human relations commission to achieve a 35 to 40 percent minority distribution among new hires.

Affirmative action plans in the paper plant have increased the flow of minorities into the upgrading system. Although total plant employment over the past five years has decreased by 10 percent, minority employment has increased by more than 6 percent. Nevertheless, upgrading of blacks to supervisory jobs remains an exception to the rule.

Government threats to cancel contracts prompted the aircraft manufacturing company to maintain and further develop comprehensive equal employment programs. The director of manufacturing assures the program's top priority by approving goals set by personnel and meeting every three months with other top management officials to insure that the goals are being met. Periodically, the program is internally audited by the equal opportunity program's director and his staff, whose work is also frequently reviewed.

In the early 1970s, this plant was criticized for its relatively low level of minorities in first-, second-, and third-level management. Despite the huge supervisory cutback at the time, a government compliance agency required the plant management's commitment to promote twenty-two black assistant foremen out of the first fifty opportunities that arose. Presently, there is no externally imposed quota, but management has taken upon itself to strive for an internally established goal. It is very likely that some less qualified minorities have been promoted to supervisory jobs because of the unrelenting pressure of the government.

Because the food plant did not begin operations until the mid-1960s, there were no past policies requiring corrective action. Government contracting, however, necessitates an affirmative action program which compels minority promotion into supervision whenever possible. The shortage of highly qualified blacks in the area makes it difficult to achieve this goal. In fact, the state employment commission has determined that the general availability of minorities having requisite skills for jobs as officials, managers, professionals, technicians, clericals, and craftsmen range from "very few" to "none."

The plant appears to be very successful in hiring minorities; total plant employment is 20 percent black, and only 11 percent of all job applicants are black. The affirmative action program does not seem to affect current upgrading procedures here as much as it affects programs that had been traditionally followed elsewhere. This is probably a result of the facility's opening at a time when illegal practices were already well known and could be avoided.

The smelter similarly does not find affirmative action plans cumbersome. Area minorities are limited, and the plant already employs a high percentage of the disadvantaged. Nevertheless, the smelter management does set annual goals. In 1972, management proposed not only an increase in the level of minority employment of one percentage point but also an audit of the skills and qualifications of minorities and females to "insure that those with potential are given opportunity for advancement to supervisory and higher level positions."

The Equal Employment Opportunity Commission pressured several of the plants to cease using tests for screening, selecting, and upgrading employees. The net effect seems to be more subjective methods of selecting supervisors in the plants. On the other hand, after meeting government requirements for validation,[3] the petroleum refinery has complied with government requirements and administers a battery of four tests to its applicants and files the results. There are no cutoff points, but a candidate is expected to obtain a "reasonable conglomerate score." It is possible that, in some cases, the test results are considered when selecting supervisors.

Throughout the paper industry, discriminatory seniority systems created artificial blocks preventing blacks from advancing into certain progression lines or restricting them to particular departments. As a result of litigation [4] and other government pressures, an "affected class" was designated at this plant, as at most southern paper plants. The class consists of all minority employees hired prior to December 31, 1969, who were initially placed in jobs which were excluded from progression lines or in jobs where the minorities constituted more than 50 percent of the incumbents. In addition, these positions frequently provided little hope of promotion.

To facilitate upward movement, the affected class agreement allows these employees to compete with each other on the basis of division rather than job seniority. For example, such a worker in the unbleached paper division can transfer or be promoted into any progression line within his division as long as he has sufficient seniority and meets or exceeds the qualifications of the least qualified employee currently in the progression

---

[3] Validation of tests is discussed in chapter VI.

[4] *United States* v. *Local 189, United Papermakers and Paperworkers et al.,* 282 F. Supp. 39 (E.D. La., 1968); *aff'd,* 416 F.2d 980 (5th Cir. 1969); *cert. denied,* 397 U.S. 919 (1970). For details of this situation, see Northrup, "The Negro in the Paper Industry," note 2 above.

line. The purpose of such a system is to minimize the effects of past discrimination on upgrading.

The advantages of such a system for the affected class are numerous, and white hourly employees and line managers have expressed considerable resentment. White hourly employees see themselves being denied jobs that they had planned to occupy. Supervisors see their loyal employees bypassed in favor of outsiders. In addition, some line managers feel that this arrangement has "clogged" the progression lines. Because some of the affected class either lack sufficient prior experience in progression line jobs or lack the education necessary to perform some top jobs, such employees have, at times, been bypassed, and less senior workers have been moved up. These less experienced workers, however, are deprived of valuable experience in the lower level positions which makes their future advancement more difficult.

As can be expected, employees at a number of the facilities studied expressed concern and resentment over the emphasis on minority promotions. For example, in the aircraft plant, management has selected blacks from the hourly ranks to be promoted into supervision, whereas comparable whites without prior supervisory experience were not selected. To meet racial goals, management was forced to do this because there were very few blacks relative to the number of whites in the pool of former supervisors from which selections were normally made. Nevertheless, one assistant foreman said, "Many employees feel there is reverse discrimination going on."

INSTITUTIONAL FACTORS

Institutional factors affecting upgrading systems are closely related to environmental ones and, like the latter, heavily affect the determination of those eligible for supervisor selection, as well as affect the system itself. The institutional factors here examined include (1) the nature of the work; (2) plant size and customs; (3) consumer market orientation; (4) the nature of the union organization; (5) management interest, action, and policy; and (6) incentives offered for the supervisory position.

The Nature of the Work

Historically, the more unpleasant the work, the greater was the availability of that work to minorities. The smelter's work is hot, heavy, and generally unpleasant. The large percentage of minorities there is directly related to this fact.

The paper, chemical, and petroleum plants all operate continuously. Workers change shifts every week. As employees grow older, many attempt to transfer into maintenance in order to avoid shift work. Such employees give up the right to bid for supervisory positions in order to avoid shift work. The desire for day work is so strong that "99 percent of the people who bid on maintenance jobs do it because of the day work involved." Not only have people accepted pay cuts of up to $1.00 per hour to be transferred to day work, but in one department where the lowest paying job is day work, employees have actually transferred down as they accumulated seniority. In fact, the foremen positions for day work, such as those in the training and maintenance departments, are considered so desirable that they are occasionally filled by lateral transfers from other departments.

When the plant attempted to use recent college graduates as foremen, the dislike for shift work kept these people from applying for jobs, and the plant was forced to revert to total reliance on hourly upgrading of those employees already working night shifts. Of course, workers generally accept promotions into higher paying night jobs.

The highly automated and sophisticated petroleum refinery, also a continuously operating plant with shifts, needs only a few employees to run large operations. The stillman position, similar to a leadman position in scope of responsibility, provides an extensive training ground for future first-line supervisors. Although it does not occur as often as in the chemical plant, day jobs in maintenance in the refinery are sometimes preferred over supervisory promotions in night shifts. Some employees, however, do prefer operations work to maintenance work because the former jobs are indoors, and the latter ones are usually out of doors.

A large portion of the black "affected class" in the paper mill were in day jobs. Many refused the upgrading because that meant going on shift work.

The food plant, operating three shifts on a fixed basis rather than on a rotating basis, faces some of the same problems as the other plants. It is very difficult for second- and third-shift people in this plant to be considered for supervisory positions because the managers responsible for evaluating their performance (upon which promotion is based) work the day shift and rarely interact with second- and third-shift workers.

When the automobile plant wants to expand production without using overtime, management can either speed up the assembly line or add a new shift. Both methods call for the creation of new supervisory positions, which provides opportunities for upgrading blue-collar hourly workers. There are, however, a number of difficulties with the second alternative. First, the existence of a second shift is uncertain and fluctuates with the economy. For example, a shift created in the early 1950s was eliminated later in the decade, only to be reinstated in the 1960s and again eliminated recently. Second, hourly employees on the first and second shift want day work rather than supervisory night positions. For example, from one hundred to two hundred applications were received for the thirty positions in the last foreman-training program, but approximately five hundred were received for eleven apprenticeship openings which lead to day work in maintenance.

The nature of the work also determines the upgrading avenues to supervision. For example, the paper industry relies on long, narrow upgrading subsystems in each of its major divisions, i.e., paper mill, pulp mill, power and recovery, and woodyard. In the paper mill, seven employees per shift operate a huge machine. Such employees work their way up the line from "No. 7," the entry position, to "machine tender," the top job. Such upgrading, based upon seniority, can take ten to fifteen years. Meanwhile, however, employees on the paper line receive no training in other divisions and, hence, cannot aspire to supervisory jobs outside of the paper mill. The same is true for those in other paper manufacturing divisions. But the top person in the hourly group in each seniority line almost always is the leading candidate for a supervisory position.

In the automobile plant, however, most jobs require comparable skills, except maintenance; therefore, seniority is virtually plantwide. Supervisory candidates are not limited to their own sector because the work throughout the plant is closely comparable.

The prerequisite skill level for many jobs at the aircraft plant and petroleum refinery is not readily available in the labor market. As a result, these facilities have instituted extensive training programs which have, in effect, limited both the number of potential candidates for top jobs and the promotion potential of workers who have not undergone this training.

The aircraft plant not only trains people for jobs when they are hired but also retrains them to meet the facility's particular manpower needs. Still, employees with deficient educational backgrounds may be unable to advance as far as they may wish. In addition to the training in specific skills, this plant also provides a voluntary evening program offering engineering and electrical courses, high school equivalency programs, college study programs, and management skill programs. Many line managers feel that the worker who takes advantage of these opportunities shows a great deal of initiative, and this is counted heavily when the worker is considered for promotion. In addition, since all supervisors are exposed to the same training program, the plant has consistent criteria upon which to rely when selecting first-line supervisors.

Consumer Market Orientation

The degree to which the product line of a company is sold directly to consumers affects the manner in which it operates and, in turn, its employee relations policies, including selection and training. Thus the automobile, petroleum, and food plant managements were made much more concerned about possible consumer impact if they were to be charged with racial or sexual discrimination than were officials in the chemical or smelter operations, which sold all their products to other producers. The consumer-oriented companies felt that supervisors should help project a "good image" and stressed this in training. Undoubtedly, this belief also affected the selection of foremen.

Plant and Size and Customs

Plant size directly affects supervisor selection systems since the smaller the plant, the more the plant's top management knows the people and participates directly in the selection process. The aircraft plant tries to overcome the disadvantages of large size through its computerized skills-inventory program. The petroleum refinery employs relatively few people, but they are dispersed over so wide an area that top management has great difficulty in knowing individuals well. In general, however, top management in the smaller plants had a much greater direct participation in the selection of foremen.

Customs developed in early plant years continue to influence the selection of supervisors. Preference and recommendations for friends and relatives when jobs open up is an established practice in the petroleum refinery (where 95 percent of all recruited hourly employees result from referrals), and until recently was standard in the smelter (a father-son tradition). Candidates are now referred to the smelter through the state employment service, but as a result of the decline in hiring, the system has not yet been tested. Line managers interviewed at the smelter felt that family-hiring patterns are carried over into promotions to supervisor.

The petroleum refinery has utilized its extensive referral system (which has contributed to maintaining a nonunion plant) to aid minority applicants, who are very active in referring their friends for work. Although upgrading has remained flexible, this referral system has at times induced the plant to hire less competent employees, who will later be unqualified for upgrading.

Unions

Although the union has an institutional life of its own, separate and distinct from a company whose employees it represents, and although unions traditionally have no voice in the actual selection of supervisory employees, whom they do not represent, unions do in fact have a profound institutional impact on procedures for selecting supervisors. For example, where, as in the paper plant and smelter, a number of craft unions exist, such demarcations add barriers to intraplant mobility and generally preclude an individual who gains his experience under one union's jurisdiction from transferring to another union's jurisdiction. Thus, his eligibility for supervision is limited to the one area.

The impact of union seniority rules on supervisor selection is particularly great, even though seniority under the union contract does not apply to supervisor selection. Companies often follow seniority in order to help keep unions out or reduce union power. Thus, the refinery is nonunion, but strict seniority in upgrading prevails and is generally followed in the selection of supervisors. In the food plant, the union is quite weak, but seniority is religiously adhered to.

Seniority rules can change selection procedure. Although in a number of the plants, such as the electrical products and chemical plants, there were originally top hourly positions designated as training grounds for future supervisors, these jobs can no longer be used in such a capacity because the unions insist on filling these according to seniority. The food plant lost a union grievance proceeding when it attempted to promote a more qualified male over a more senior female into such a position. The paper plant faces a similar problem.

Only the automobile and aircraft plants maintain a degree of flexibility in the area of seniority. The automobile assembly line, horizontal by nature, does not require union rigidity on the issue. The facility has enjoyed a good union-management relationship and experiences a relatively low grievance rate. Of course, this does not imply a weak union. The plant is organized by the United Auto Workers, and because of the facility's limited three-day material stockpile, the union maintains a good deal of leverage. This plant, like the food plant, fills the leadman position by seniority.

The aircraft plant deals with a much weaker union and retains flexibility in layoffs. It has instituted a system of transfer in lieu of layoff whereby less senior employees are not necessarily bumped by more senior workers. Cutbacks are controlled by plantwide seniority within job classifications and grades. When an employee is selected for layoff, he may apply (upon agreement from plant management) for a transfer, which is usually awarded to the most senior employee. Thus, the plant both retains its best workers and provides protection for more senior employees. This is also a protection for the plant's minority workers, who are generally lower in seniority ranking. The program, however, results in many promotion rejections in times of layoffs because some senior employees in lower grades feel that their present positions provide more job security than higher grades provide. Because supervisors are chosen from grade-one workers, potential upgrading into supervision for employees who reject promotions is also effectively delayed. (See Table III-2 for a summary of hourly upgrading procedures.)

Unions can also greatly reduce the job security of supervisors and, thus, cause employees to refuse such promotions. Only the nonunion petroleum workers and those in the aircraft plant retain seniority in the hourly ranks after promotion to supervisor. Union contracts deny this protection in the other plants.

At the smelter, the union not only controls the seniority system, a situation creating a barrier to upgrading, but also controls the amount of supervisor training a potential foreman may receive while still an hourly worker. Because an hourly worker in the training position receives a 15 percent higher wage, the union negotiated a thirty-day per year limit on the amount of time an hourly may train in such work. During this time and for forty-eight hours after his last shift in this position, the employee is prohibited from working overtime.

Despite these union restrictions, several of the plants feel that union officials have, by their service, indicated leadership ability, and this counts in their favor during supervisor selection.

Management Interest, Action, and Policy

Despite all other factors, management interest, action, and policy can tremendously affect supervisor selection. Concern by top management about upgrading procedure can result in improvement and change in the procedure. The opposite is also true. Thus, when the parent company took over direct management of the smelter, there was for the first time in many years interest expressed in improving supervisor selection and staff assistance for that purpose; the disinterest of the central headquarters of the paper company has, despite valiant efforts by the personnel executive, been reflected at the plant level.

The aerospace facility has long had a strong personnel executive who has instituted procedures for selecting supervisors and made certain that they are given importance and weight by the line; the central management of the automobile assembly plant has made it clear to plant management that supervisor selection programs are mandatory and will be supported financially and otherwise. On the other hand, new management in the food company appears less interested in personnel matters than its predecessors appeared, a trend which will undoubtedly be reflected in supervisor-upgrading programs at the plant level.

We could cite many other examples from our research which, like the above, point to the crucial role of management interest in the selection and upgrading procedure.

Incentives

The type and quantity of incentives offered to workers who are candidates for supervisory positions certainly influence the quantity and quality of the applicants, as well as their enthusiasm and satisfaction. Most plants offer both financial and psychological incentives.

TABLE III-2
Upgrading: Hourly Promotions

Plant	Division	Seniority	Progression Lines	Method to Publicize Positions	Training	Transfers	Union Status
Nonferrous Smelter	O	Very rigid.	Very rigid.	Posting 7 days; bids.		First choice from within dept.; 7-day posting; bids; job goes to highest seniority.	Very strong; "tough," "adamant," "militant" relationship with management.
	M	Follows from apprenticeship.	Follows from apprenticeship.		Apprenticeship tests, schooling.		
Paper Manufacturer	O P	Rigid.	Rigid, long, narrow.	Requests with forms and interviews; many more maintenance than operations requests.	On-the-job with progression line not formal.	Superintendent selects from those recommended; seniority given preference.	Strong insistence on seniority; used as stepping stone to supervision.
	M	Used for promotion.	Limited, but used for promotion.		Apprenticeship or outside craftsman.		
Automobile Assembly Plant	O	Firm unless another worker far superior.	Very limited; horizontal line.	Posting; inquire whether senior employees want it; form.		Transfer form.	Very strong, but not harassing.
	M	Formal selection; emphasis more on ability, less on seniority.	Apprenticeship.	Posting; test; interview.	Apprenticeship, 4 years; employee-in-training, 8 years.	Based on ability, potential, seniority; joint union-management selection committee.	

Aircraft Manu-facturer		Governs wherever fitness and ability are equal.	No progression lines; organized by job classifi-cation.	Requests filed with internal placement, screened.	Voluntary; tech-nical training.	Open transfer; internal place-ment office.	Not particularly strong; not a stepping stone.
Electrical Products Manu-facturer	O	Completely governs.	No progression lines; job classi-fication.	Posting 24 hours.		Eligible after 1 year's service; requests consid-ered if no unit employee responds to posted notice.	Extremely power-ful; not a stepping stone.
	M	Usually governs.	Job classification according to training.		No program; hired with 6 years' relevant experi-ence or appren-ticeship 4 years.		
Chemical Manu-facturer	O	Strong seniority.	No progression lines; departments with classifi-cations.	Posting 2 weeks.	Operations train-ing; technical subjects.	Based on senior-ity within smallest unit.	Strong insistence on departmental and unit senior-ity; used as a stepping stone.
	L	Flexible seniority.	Apprenticeship.		Lab training for promotion.		
	M	Flexible seniority.	Apprenticeship.	Posting; bids.	Four-year appren-ticeship classroom.		
Food Processing Plant	O	Seniority generally rules.	No progression lines; 17 func-tional depart-ments.	Posting; bids 3 days.	Little; most jobs semiskilled.	Requests between shifts between depts.; seniority important.	Not particularly strong in general; has achieved a strong seniority system; stepping stone.
	M	Based on ability.	No progression lines; experience rules.		Limited appren-ticeship; experi-ence necessary.		

TABLE III-2 (continued)

Plant	Division	Seniority	Progression Lines	Method to Publicize Positions	Training	Transfers	Union Status
Petroleum Refinery	O	Strong seniority; seniority within departments.	Limited progression lines; job categories.	Posting.	Elaborate training, 3 years; commitment, 7 years.	Posting; bids; requests.	No union.
	M	Seniority governs until training undergone.			Training, 8,000 hours.		

Key: O = Operations.
M = Maintenance.
L = Laboratory.
P = Power.

Financial Incentives. As shown in Table III-3, all but two of the eight plants studied use salary increases to encourage new employees to accept promotion. The chemical plant maintains a $200 per month differential between the foreman's and hourly's wages. If the foreman is on a rotating shift, he receives an additional 15 percent of his base income and is paid time and one-half for scheduled overtime. There is considerable opportunity to advance to second- and third-level management.

Although money was not mentioned as an incentive for promotion in the food plant, this is again attributable to the satisfactory wage differential maintained between the hourly and supervisory work forces. The automobile plant, however, has encountered problems with its wage scale. Although it maintains a minimum 25 percent base wage differential, production workers' overtime can narrow the gap substantially.

The major financial problems occur in the electrical products plant, where the hourly incentive pay system allows an hourly employee to produce at an efficiency rate of 200 to 300 percent and earn from 30 to 60 percent more than the base rate. It was reported that an average first-line supervisor earns about $10,500 per year, while some hourly employees make as much as $14,000 to $15,000 and occasionally even $19,000 per year. Moreover, although the first-line supervisors have a better life insurance program than the hourly employees, most other fringe benefits favor hourly workers. It is not surprising, then, that the electrical plant encounters serious difficulties in attracting supervisors from the hourly ranks.

The petroleum refinery, when experiencing an upsurge of business, also found that many hourly workers earn more with overtime than foremen earn. Although this is a temporary situation, it can easily inhibit workers from seeking promotion. Money is a prime incentive to accepting higher level jobs. Once that issue is met, then other incentives enter the picture.

Psychological Incentives. A person's desires for advancement, prestige, status, achievement, and challenging work can be satisfied with a promotion from hourly work to the ranks of supervision and management. Hourly employees are well aware of the foreman's opportunities and view promotion as a large step forward. As Table III-3 demonstrates, these factors both motivate workers to accept advancement and are their major sources of satisfaction with the work in their new capacities. Moreover, many foremen indicated that they enjoy working with many

TABLE III-3
*Attitudes of Former Hourly Workers Toward
Their Promotions and Work in Supervisory Positions*

Variable	Aircraft Manuf.	Chemical Manuf.	Food Processing Plant	Electrical Products Manuf.	Paper Manuf.	Nonferrous Smelter	Automobile Assembly Plant	Petroleum Refinery
Incentives								
Financial	X	X			X	X	X	X
Advancement	X	X	X	X	X	X	X	
Challenge of Work	X					X	X	
Other	Working with people; exercising authority.	Status.	Working with people; achieving personal goals.	Prestige; variety of work; ordered to accept job; desire to better oneself; 75% tuition rebate.		Prestige; pride; personal goals; frequent union strikes.	Working with people; prestige; upward mobility.	X
Satisfaction								
Financial	X	X						
Advancement		X						
Challenge of Work	X		X	X		X	X	X
Other	Variety of experience; being a leader; accomplishment.		Variety of work; working with people; prestige; accomplishment.	Variety of work; accomplishment; seeing results.		Variety of work; accomplishment; working with people.	Working with people.	Pressures; strong management support.

	Dissatisfaction: Excessive Paperwork	Shift Work	Poor Management Relations	Little Official Support	Insufficient Authority	Other	Promotion: Rejections Are a Problem	Reasons: Fear of Responsibility	Pressures	Other
		X	X			Transition from hourly work hard; loss of friends; worker harassment.		X	X	Shift work; relative easiness of some jobs.
				X	X	Insufficient wage differential; troublesome union.	X		X	Union membership; lack of money; lack of managerial support.
						Equipment problems; overtime; bad worker attitude.	X			Religion, health requirement; inadequate pay.
			X	X		Insufficient pay; indifference of superiors to foremen; more concern with neighborhood than with properly running the plant.				Lack of financial incentive.
		X	X			Insufficient pay relative to amount of work.		X		
	X		X		X			X	X	More security as a union member.

people and like the variety of work offered by the supervisory job as opposed to the monotony of work which usually characterizes hourly jobs. The supervisors also enjoy taking on greater responsibility and authority.

The sources of dissatisfaction with work are also psychological. Many foremen indicated a lack of management support as a major problem. In the food plant, for example, although management increases the prestige of the job by giving supervisors a distinctive hat and allowing them to eat in the management dining room, management is accused of showing no respect for foremen because it emphasizes "production at any cost."

The foremen in the automobile plant also feel that they are neither given enough authority nor respected enough. They admit, however, that, as a result of some new training programs for general foremen and above, the relationship with higher management has begun to improve.

The situation in the petroleum refinery is just the opposite. Management makes outstanding efforts to take an interest in the employees. Top officials personally welcome new hourly employees, and the personnel office constantly meets with workers to learn of any difficulties or grievances. In addition, any accomplishments of workers' families are formally recognized. Management's strong interest in the employees has both helped to keep the plant nonunion and created a strong worker loyalty. This has allowed more flexibility for management and has encouraged a low rejection rate for upgrading offers.

CONCLUSIONS

The promotion systems utilized at the various plants may be informal, but they are not randomly established. Environmental and institutional factors impose constraints on the systems desired, and the results are often attributable to exogenous variables which affect the system, such as historical events, economic conditions, and government policies.

A plant developing a promotion system must take all factors into account and work within the framework provided by the available work force and the nature of the work performed in the particular industry. The work dictates certain progression lines and certain restrictions on the qualifications of workers who are potential candidates for promotion. By insisting on seniority and plant customs, the union dictates certain restrictions on management's flexibility in hiring and promotion. The corporation, through expansions and contractions in the plants and work force, enhances or limits promotion opportunities. In addition, through the working relationships that are maintained between hourly workers and foremen and through the various types of incentives that are provided for workers seeking promotion, the corporation can encourage or discourage workers from seeking upgrading. When hourly jobs provide greater job security, higher wages, and fewer frustrations, an employee will be very tempted to overlook promotion opportunities.

The model for these systems, then, as indicated previously, is an interactive model which cannot provide any regular, patterned outcome. Therefore, a plant may be forced to run a less efficient or desirable personnel system with the knowledge that, although it is far from the best system, it is the *best possible*, given the existing constraints. It is here that an additional influence on the system comes into play. Outside of the environmental and institutional factors guiding upgrading selections, there are personal variables that differentiate those workers who are upgraded from hourly jobs into supervision from those who are not offered promotion opportunities. Although seniority generally governs hourly promotions, when it comes to supervisors, the selection becomes more important, and those making the selection seek certain qualities that they feel are characteristic of a good supervisor. The next chapter discusses those differentiating variables.

CHAPTER IV

Personal Factors and Selection Criteria

Besides the environmental and institutional factors which affect supervisor selection are the personal characteristics of the candidates. We hypothesized that there are quantifiable personal characteristics that distinguish those selected as supervisors from those who remain hourly workers. This hypothesis is examined in the first part of this chapter. The second part of the chapter analyzes the various selection criteria which were reported in the interviews described in chapter II.

PERSONAL FACTORS

Personal data on workers were gathered from random samples of employee personnel files to ascertain whether this quantifiable information can be used to distinguish objectively between hourly and supervisory workers. Various statistical tests were performed on each set of data from the plants to accomplish this task.[1]

There was some discrepancy in the availability of information from plant to plant. Although most facilities always maintained detailed records on every employee, there were some exceptions. The nonferrous smelter, for example, had very incomplete records because of a change in ownership which was accompanied by a change in personnel methods. As a result, it did not have sufficient quantifiable data by which to predict accurately which workers were most likely to become supervisors. Yet certain variables were more significant than others in distinguishing between the two groups.

---

[1] The detailed results and statistical manipulation tables for each plant are on file in the Industrial Research Unit library and are also found in William E. Fulmer, "Becoming a Supervisor: A Study of Personal Characteristics and Other Factors that Impact on the Process of Upgrading Workers to Supervision" (Ph.D. diss., University of Pennsylvania, 1974).

The aircraft plant, unlike the other facilities, did not gather the personal data from historical records, but instead collected it from the skills inventory program that had been instituted. Consequently, the available data differed in some areas from that of other plants and is not as complete in some aspects. Most facilities quantified ten or eleven variables for testing. The chemical plant was able to quantify sixteen variables, but the quality of the data was not very good.

The first statistical test performed on each set of data was a univariate test on means which was designed to ascertain whether there were actual differences between the quantified variables of hourly and supervisory workers. For each plant (except the smelter), significant differences between the populations were found. Because a univariate test on means does not take into account interactions of variables, a discriminant analysis on these variables was also performed. The results of this test were also generally quite good; misclassifications of individuals as hourly workers or as supervisors were not too common. .

Some of the data collected were eliminated from these tests. For example, current age was often not included for testing because it generally correlates highly with years of seniority. In the automobile plant, the number of dependents was also excluded from analysis since it showed a very high correlation with age. The test results at the food plant were the most significant of all the results and predicted future foremen with the most accuracy.

Two more statistical tests were run on the data to identify precisely which variables were most important in distinguishing between the groups: a stepwise discriminant analysis and the more conservative simultaneous confidence intervals test. The latter test provided a more rigorous analysis and often found variables insignificant although the former test found them significant. Table IV-1 indicates which tests provided the results presented, as well as the variables that were significant at each plant.

Seniority

Even under the more rigorous statistical analysis (see Table IV-1), it is not at all surprising that seniority stands out as a major factor in discriminating between hourly and supervisory employees at almost all the plants. Most supervisory jobs require a comprehensive knowledge of the production processes and machinery which the foreman is to supervise. This knowledge can

TABLE IV-1
*Variables Distinguishing
Hourly from Supervisory Workers*

Variable	Automobile Assembly Plant	Electrical Products Manuf.	Food Processing Plant	Chemical Manuf.	Petroleum Refinery	Nonferrous Smelter	Paper Manuf.	Aircraft Manuf.
Personal								
Current Seniority	XS		XS	X	XS	X	XS	X
Years of Education	X	XS	XS	X	X		X	XS
Number of Organization Memberships	X	X	XS			XS		
Number of Jobs Held in Last Five Years	X		X			X	X	X
Number of Relatives and Friends Employed Here		X	X			XS		
Number of Permanent Jobs Held at Plant			XS		X		XS	XS
Test Scores							X	
Miscellaneous								
Sex	X		X					X
Race	X		X				X	X
Marital Status	X		X	X	X		X	X
Military Service	X					X	X	X
Military Rank	X					X		
Military Discharge								
Residence					X			
Referral Source	X				X			

Key: S = Significance by simultaneous confidence intervals. X = Significance by stepwise discriminant analysis.

best be gained by experience on the job. Hence, especially in plants with lengthy progression lines, there is a wide discrepancy in the average number of years of seniority between the employee groups. In the petroleum refinery, for example, the average foreman has thirty years of seniority; the average hourly worker has only fifteen. The foremen, in addition, usually are selected from the tops of their progression lines. As a result both of this reason and of union pressures, foremen are usually the most senior employees.

In plants like the automobile facility, of course, the progression lines are wider and shorter. There, too, the more senior people occupy supervisory positions. The reason is twofold: (1) the computed seniority average is low as a result of very high turnover among hourly workers; and (2) model changes are very difficult and necessitate direction from a foreman who has had much experience in the area.

The food plant also presents an interesting case. First-line supervisors tend to have eight and one-half years of seniority, whereas hourly workers have about five. The average supervisor's age at hire, however, is relatively low. This situation exists because the plant has tended to promote its original work force to supervision (the plant has been open only a few years), and it also has attempted to employ recent college graduates as foremen.

The petroleum plant probably shows the most significant results from the analysis of employee seniority. With that information alone, management could distinguish between hourly and supervisory employees in 88.4 percent of the cases. Foremen tend to have more seniority than hourly workers not only because of the importance of seniority in the progression lines but also because of the layoffs in the early 1960s which left only the more senior employees in the work force. Also, the refinery rewards loyal employees with promotions. Loyalty is frequently manifested through many years of work at the plant.

Education

The educational level of supervisors is generally much higher than that of the average hourly worker. Managements in the petroleum refinery, automobile plant, and chemical facility indicated that they heavily emphasize intelligence (as measured by years of schooling) and initiative (as measured by the desire for more education).

For three of the plants, education is a significant factor even under the more rigorous statistical analysis (see Table IV-1). The food plant attempts to maintain a certain proportion of first-line supervisors who are college graduates, which accounts for the difference between hourlies' and foremen's years of education. The electrical products plant experiences a high rejection rate of promotion offers and often must hire supervisors from the outside instead of upgrade hourly workers. As long as management employs outsiders for supervisors, it prefers to hire those with more education. In addition, first-line supervisors at the food plant often take advantage of the tuition refund program.

For the aircraft plant, education is one of the two most significant variables differentiating between hourly and supervisory workers. Here, the finding is largely attributable to the high level of requisite skill for the specialized work. All first-line supervisors have high school diplomas, two have bachelor's degrees, and one even has a master of arts.

Although education does differentiate between the two groups in the other plants, it is not a particularly significant variable. In both the paper plant and the petroleum refinery, for example, there is little difference in schooling, but that is probably attributable to less emphasis placed on education at the time that the first-line supervisors were young. In addition, the foremen were about college age during the Depression, when responsibility was geared toward family support and not toward educational enrichment. Because of the nature of the work involved, the chemical plant requires a high school education of all new hires, and the smelter, for a few years, followed a policy of hiring more educated workers. Consequently, the schooling differential between the two groups at the above facilities is relatively small.

We see then that education does discriminate between hourly and supervisory workers, but the differential is not always large or particularly significant. It generally depends on the type of work to be performed and the personnel policies followed at the individual facilities.

Organization Memberships

The factor of organization memberships is significant in distinguishing hourly from supervisory workers in only four plants, and only in the food plant and the smelter is membership in organizations significant under the more rigorous statistical analysis. In all but the automobile plant, supervisory workers tend to belong to more organizations than hourly workers do.

This characteristic may be indicative of a number of things. First, it probably implies a greater inclination of supervisors toward social interaction. This is an important trait because a foreman must be able to get along well with others. Second, this trait may indicate a greater leadership ability, which is also important for a foreman.

In both the food and electrical products plants, there are a relatively large number of college graduates in supervisory positions. It is not surprising that these people belong to a large number of organizations, since many were fraternity brothers and participated in professional groups during college.

One may fairly conclude that the high positive correlation between organization memberships and work position is to be expected, given the requisites for success as a supervisor.

Job History

Although for any of the plants job history is not significant under analysis with the conservative confidence intervals test, the less stringent stepwise discriminant analysis points toward its importance in five of the eight facilities; the number of permanent jobs held during the five years prior to work at the plant is particularly important in three facilities.

In general, supervisors had both worked for longer periods of time on the last job prior to work at the plant and held fewer jobs in the five years before working at their present positions. The only exception to this is the automobile plant, where the reverse is true. The general situation is probably indicative of a greater stability and sense of responsibility, two essential traits for a foreman. We may postulate that the automobile plant's supervisory force was less stable than most when first hired as hourly workers, but it had also taken them longer to reach their present position (nine years).

It is interesting to note that, in the aircraft plant, the average first-line supervisor began to work at age twenty-five, whereas the typical hourly worker began working at twenty-eight. This was a direct result of the plant expansion, during which many young hourly workers were promoted to supervision. Proving their abilities by strong performances, they were retained later on during the period of contraction.

Foremen had generally held more permanent jobs at the same facility than had hourly workers. Theoretically, such a background provides them with more experience and familiarizes them with all aspects of the plant. Consequently, these people are better prepared for supervision. Only in the petroleum refinery was the reverse situation true, presumably because most of the supervisors had been working in such a capacity for almost seven years.

A note of caution is appropriate here. Not all the data are reliable; it was found that not all supervisors interpreted and answered all the questions in the same manner. For example, in the aircraft plant, when asked to list the number of jobs performed in the facility, some included their present position and some did not. In addition, the stricter statistical test did not always point to a significant difference.

Friends and Relatives

In both the smelter and the electrical products plant, foremen are found to be friendly with significantly fewer people and to have fewer relatives at the plant than are the hourly workers. There are a number of factors that could account for this.

At the electrical plant, there is considerable difficulty attracting hourly workers to supervisory positions. Consequently, most first-line supervisors are "outsiders" and enter without prior connections. In the smelter, there are a number of college graduates who also entered not knowing many people. In addition, it appears that the fewer friends a worker has, the less he is dependent on others to "lash out for him." He tends, therefore, to be more ambitious and self-sufficient and "fools around" much less than other workers. This type of behavior often impresses management, and such a worker is promoted.

The average foreman in the electrical products plant had twice as many children as the average hourly worker had at the time of hire, a fact perhaps reflecting a greater maturity. This is inconclusive, however, given that the average hourly worker was employed at twenty-seven years of age, while the average foreman did not begin service until he was thirty.

Test Scores

Only the paper plant manifests differences in test scores between foremen and supervisors, and the difference is not statistically significant (partially attributable to the small sample size). In addition, because the tests are not universally applied, the results cannot be used as a basis of comparison.

Miscellaneous Variables

Eight miscellaneous variables were analyzed to determine their significance in differentiating hourly from supervisory employees. It appears that certain variables, such as marital status, race, sex, and military service often are significant. One could intuitively realize a logical reason why marital status and military service are important. A person who marries early is often considered more mature, responsible, and stable than his peers. He is, therefore, more likely to be successful as a supervisor. Military service is a good training ground for these qualities, and serving as an officer is indicative of leadership abilities. It is no surprise that workers with these attributes are often the same people chosen for supervision. Only at the automobile plant had more hourly workers been officers than had supervisors.

Racial and sexual differences between the groups are important because they often reflect the institutional and environmental factors discussed in the earlier chapters. Where the work is less pleasant and more physical, fewer women are employed, and consequently, few are promoted. If past hiring practices were discriminatory (as they often were), we would not expect the minority groups or females to have acquired sufficient seniority or experience to qualify them for promotion. In addition, minorities often have had less education, have not scored as high on tests, and have had inferior job performance records. Such a situation prevails in the food plant, in the paper mill, and in the petroleum refinery.

Generally, if referral source is significant, most foremen were referred from outside sources and did not have inside connections. When residence is indicated as an important variable, foremen either owned their own homes (paper plant) or else rented rather than lived with relatives upon hire (petroleum refinery). Both these traits show independence and self-reliance, again, two important characteristics for a foreman.

One qualification must be made concerning these data. The information does not always reflect the obvious. For example, one explanation of why there are more supervisors than hourly workers (at the smelter) who were in the service is that the age differential between the groups placed supervisors at the draft age for World War II, but placed hourly workers at draft age only after the war was over. In the food plant, however, there is no difference in age, and yet, supervisors did have more military experience. Nevertheless, one must be aware of the potential pitfalls of the data.

Miscellaneous variables, then, had different effects in different facilities and are subject to fairly simple explanations for their significance. Generally, we find that the characteristics indicative of a responsible, stable, mature, and independent person are more likely to be found in the supervisory work force than in the hourly work force, and reasonably so.

Final Comments

This section quite clearly indicates that one may draw general conclusions about the type of people who are more likely to be selected for supervisory positions and those who are more likely to remain hourly workers. There are two groups of personal miscellaneous variables which are significant in this respect: characteristics which are not under a person's control, such as sex or race; and personality or indigenous characteristics which are likely to vary over time, such as military experience, marital status, residence conditions, and referral source.

It appears that foremen exhibit more of the traits that indicate responsibility, stability, and ambition. They usually are more educated, were married earlier, and were active in leadership positions before working at the plant. Other variables are not easily controlled by the workers. Females and minorities, for example, are inherently placed at a disadvantage with regard to promotion, often because of the nature of the work and its physical and skill requirements and often because of past hiring and institutional practices of the plant. Nevertheless, when carefully considered, these findings are not surprising. The foreman's work, because of its requirements and expectations, necessitates a particular type of person—at least in the minds of those who select him.

SELECTION CRITERIA

After completing each of the eight field visits conducted during the course of the study, the authors compiled and analyzed the various selection criteria which had been reported in interviews at the various plants. (See chapter II for a description of the process.) Any criterion that had been identified approximately 30 percent of the time either by the first-line supervisors or by the higher management personnel that were interviewed was arbitrarily defined as a major criterion and was added to a list along with its respective definition.

These lists were incorporated into two forms: one to be used for evaluating hourly and supervisory employees by the listed criteria and the second to be used in establishing an average ranking for each characteristic in order of its importance as a criterion for selecting supervisors. Appendix E provides samples of the forms, the criteria, and their definitions.

Results: Comparison of Forced Rankings by Foremen and Supervisors

The results of the forced rankings (see Table IV-2) differ appreciably from those of the rankings that are based on frequency of suggestion during plant interviews. For example, although getting along with people was consistently mentioned in interviews as an important consideration, it scores very low in the forced rankings. Leadership, on the other hand, scores considerably higher in the forced rankings than in the frequency rankings. Perhaps the difference can be explained by the fact that, although human relations skills are commonly considered in the selection process, they do not receive the emphasis that their frequency of reporting indicates. Instead, greater emphasis is placed on characteristics that indicate leadership potential. Only at the aircraft plant, where there were only five criteria to be ranked, and where there is a strong emphasis on affirmative action which might contribute to a greater emphasis on human relations skills, did first-line supervisors rank getting along with people higher than fifth. Another indication of the general lack of emphasis on human relations skills is the small difference between the average profile for all first-line supervisors and all hourly employees. The gap of one-half of one point (0.5) is the smallest for any criterion.

Aside from the major criteria mentioned above, there is some inconsistency between the significance allotted different variables by foremen and higher management. For example, for the food plant, the higher the level of management ranking the characteristics, the less emphasis placed on performance and the more placed on initiative and education. The same holds true for the paper plant and the chemical plant; similarly, the aircraft managers rely heavily on job knowledge.

TABLE IV-2
Foremen's and Higher Management's
Forced Rankings of Selection Criteria

Variable	Paper Manuf.	Aircraft Manuf.	Electrical Products Manuf.	Chemical Manuf.	Food Processing Plant	Petroleum Refinery
Leadership	2.4[a]/2.6[b]		1.6/1.2	1.7/1.6	2.4/2.1	3.0/2.4
Good Health	3.8/5.3					
Attitude	3.8/3.8	2.7/3.5				3.0/3.8
Job Knowledge	4.0/4.4	4.0/3.2	3.4/2.0	4.6/6.1	3.6/3.6	3.4/3.8
Ability to Get Along with People	4.0/4.2	2.7/2.6	5.0/5.0	5.7/5.3	—/5.4	4.2/4.2
Initiative	5.9/3.0	1.7/2.2	3.8/5.2	5.1/3.3	—/3.6	
Fairness	—/4.9					
Past Work Record		3.9/3.6				
Intelligence			3.6/4.0	3.9/3.9	—/4.0	
Strong Character			5.6/4.5			
Dependability			5.0/6.0	4.0/4.6		3.9/3.2
Cooperative				5.8/5.9		
Job Performance				4.6/5.4	—/4.2	
Dedication					—/5.0	
Common Sense						3.5/3.5

Note: This table summarizes more complete data presented in Appendix F. Although more than two management groups participated in the forced ranking, only two were chosen for this table.

[a]Foremen's rankings.

[b]Higher management's rankings.

Of importance is that selection criteria rankings of the average hourly employee and the average first-line supervisor differ the most at those plants where there is a stronger tendency to employ college graduates as supervisors. This seems particularly true for the criterion of leadership. Although this may indicate that college-trained supervisors are better leaders, it also may reflect greater opportunities to demonstrate leadership potential or perhaps quite different value judgments and perceptions.

Comparison of Supervisors and Hourly Workers

A profile comparison shows that foremen are generally perceived as superior to hourly employees along the major criteria for supervisor selection. As Figure IV-1 demonstrates, whereas first-line supervisors are most often evaluated as exhibiting the pertinent characteristics, these same characteristics are only mildly descriptive of hourly employees, whose scores tend to center about the middle of the scale (2.5-3.0). It appears from the scores that supervisors were very reluctant to label anyone below average on any particular trait.

Except for the aircraft manufacturing company, in which it was not included, leadership is identified in the plants as the most important quality for a first-line supervisor to possess. In addition, when comparing average scores on profiles of each of the criteria in Figure IV-1, the greatest gap apparently pertains to leadership. Generally, it is for this criterion that the gap between foremen and hourly workers is in excess of one point.

Final Comments

In general, line management tends to perceive first-line supervisors as superior to hourly employees in terms of the important criteria that usually are used to evaluate potential supervisors, particularly leadership. It is this same quality that comes out on top in the forced rankings. The other attributes mentioned, such as attitude, initiative, dependability, and fairness, are logically related to leadership and would probably be found in a person who manifests leadership qualities. Job knowledge is not accorded the importance one might expect. In order to reach a management position, however, some basic level of job knowledge is important. After one reaches a certain level, other factors become more dominant.

FIGURE IV-1
Profile Comparison for Hourly and Supervisory Workers

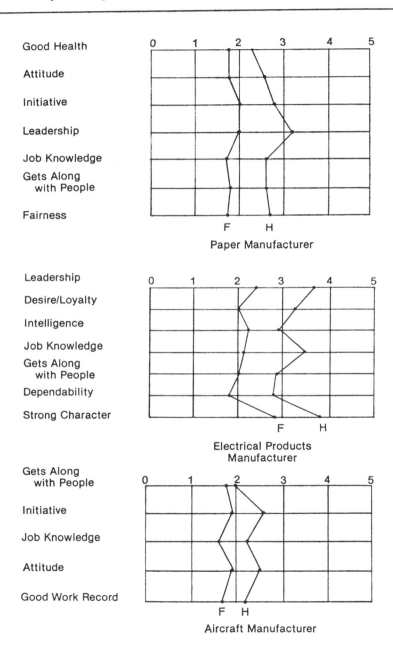

Paper Manufacturer

Electrical Products
Manufacturer

Aircraft Manufacturer

Leadership

Attitude/
  Loyalty

Job Knowledge

Dependability/
  Responsibility

Gets Along
  with People

Common Sense

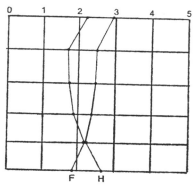

Petroleum Refinery

Leadership

Dependability/
  Responsibility

Intelligence

Job Knowledge

Cooperation

Job Performance

Gets Along
  with People

Initiative

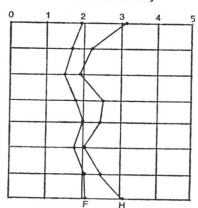

Chemical Manufacturer

Initiative

Job Knowledge

Gets Along
  with People

Leadership

Dedication

Education/
  Intelligence

Job Performance

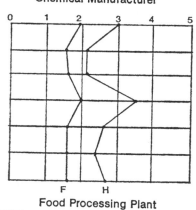

Food Processing Plant

Key: F = First-line supervisors.
     H = Hourly workers.

CHAPTER V

Industrial Supervisor Selection Practices Concluding Remarks

In order to understand American industry's practices of selecting supervisors, we examined in detail the procedures and policies in eight plants, each in a different industry and each with a distinct upgrading and selection procedure. Answers to three basic questions were sought:

1. How are people upgraded into first-level supervisory positions?
2. What factors significantly affect the operation of the upgrading process?
3. What are the characteristics of the people who tend to be upgraded into supervision?

We assume—and we believe reasonably—that the eight plants studied are typical and representative of American industry, and that our results can properly be generalized.

HOW PEOPLE ARE UPGRADED TO SUPERVISORY POSITIONS

As frequently noted, the process for selecting supervisors is generally a very informal group process controlled by management. Only three of the eight plants utilize informal, written procedures to aid the selection process, and only one of the three reports following written procedures consistently.

The analysis indicates that the common selection procedures are dictated by line management, usually the department heads. Consequently, the procedures that are followed often differ among departments within the same plant. Nevertheless, some consistencies are apparent. For example, the second and third lines of management usually exercise the most power in the selection decision. Although the first-line supervisor is occasionally consulted informally for recommendations and in some cases has a crucial input into the decision, he rarely plays a key role in the selection decision. In addition, higher management levels generally only review and approve the recommendations made by the second and third levels of management.

The actual selection decision is usually reached at an informal meeting of second- and third-line management. If there is any disagreement, the third-level manager's opinion most often prevails. Another fairly common procedure involves the second-level manager's developing a list of two or three possible candidates and ranking them in order of acceptability. This list is then submitted to the third-level manager, who reviews it, perhaps discusses it with his subordinate, and then either approves or disapproves the recommendation. Although the upgrading of hourly employees to supervision is controlled by line management, personnel officials are almost always involved in the process as advisors on the strengths and weaknesses of the candidates and on current affirmative action commitments.

Where plants do not consistently follow formal selection procedures, the supervisor selection process tends to be an extension of the hourly upgrading process. In the five such plants examined in the study, the first-line supervisors often come from the top hourly jobs in the respective lines of progression or departments. Of the three plants in which there are no specific positions from which hourly employees usually enter supervision, two have major problems with rejections of promotions to supervision. The remaining plant consistently follows a formal selection process.

In general, procedures for selecting supervisors have been relatively neglected. Top management officials frequently express concern over the people who are upgraded to supervision, but rarely express concern over the method by which they are selected. The result is informal selection procedures, the details of which are frequently unknown to top management.

Criteria for Selection

Table V-1 summarizes the selection criteria that were identified in the plant interviews by first-line supervisors and members of higher management. In many plants, the first-line supervisors are frequently consulted when supervisors are selected.

TABLE V-1
Summary of Supervisor Selection Criteria

Plant	First-Line Supervisors	Higher Management
Paper Manufacturer	Ability to get along with people Job knowledge Attitude Leadership Fairness Honesty Ability to communicate Initiative Seniority Planning ability Reliability	Ability to get along with people Technical competence Leadership Good health Initiative Loyalty Ability to communicate Reliability Confidence Education Good judgment Administrative ability Morality, honesty
Nonferrous Smelter	Initiative, dependability Job knowledge Ability to get along with people Leadership Attitude Character Intelligence Safety consciousness	Ability to get along with people Job knowledge Initiative Leadership Intelligence, education Safety and absentee record Health Responsibility Age
Aircraft Manufacturer	Ability to get along with people Good work record Initiative, drive Job knowledge Attitude, company loyalty Intelligence, education Leadership Appearance Adaptability Ability to communicate	Ability to get along with people Technical ability Attitude Initiative Age, seniority Absentee record Physical ability
Food Processing Plant	Initiative Leadership Ability to get along with people Job knowledge Job performance Patience Attitude Appearance Decisiveness	Initiative Leadership Job performance Ability to get along with people Dedication Education, intelligence Job knowledge
Automobile Assembly Plant	Ability to get along with people Drive, aggressiveness Attitude, loyalty Dependability Patience Firmness	Ability to get along with people Job knowledge Drive, motivation Fairness Intelligence, education
Electrical Products Manufacturer	Desire, initiative Job knowledge Leadership Dependability	Strong character, decisiveness Job knowledge Leadership Intelligence

TABLE V-1 (continued)

Plant	First-Line Supervisors	Higher Management
	Ability to get along with people Intelligence Good personality	
Chemical Manufacturer	Ability to get along with people Dependability, responsibility Job knowledge, mechanical ability Ability to make suggestions	Ability to get along with people Leadership Job knowledge, mechanical ability Initiative Intelligence Job performance Dependability, responsibility Cooperation Ability to communicate Judgment
Petroleum Refinery	Job knowledge Ability to get along with people Leadership Dependability, responsibility Emotional stability	Attitude, loyalty Ability to get along with people Job knowledge Leadership Common sense Intelligence

Since they also currently work in such a capacity, it was felt that they would have valuable insights into the characteristics an employee should possess in order to handle the job, although members of higher management usually make the final selection.

Employees who are upgraded to first-line supervisory positions are usually screened by several levels of management. Frequently, the criteria that are emphasized by one level differ from the criteria used by another (see Table V-1). In addition, there are important variations between plants. For example, management at the electrical products manufacturer wants supervisors who have "strong characters" and are decisive; the petroleum refinery's management emphasizes an employee's attitude and loyalty to the company. The difference can probably be explained by the different circumstances surrounding the two plants. Whereas the electrical products management deals with a relatively strong union, the petroleum refinery is nonunion, and its management works to retain that status.

Despite the variations between plants and between levels of management within the same plant, there are remarkable consistencies in the reported criteria (see Table V-2). All of the criteria shown in Table V-2 were identified in at least five of the eight plants. As the table indicates, there are four criteria consistently emphasized by all levels of management and by at least three-fourths of the plants included in this study: ability to get along with people, job knowledge, leadership, and initiative. It seems that first-line supervisors place considerable emphasis on dependability and attitude, while higher management emphasizes education and/or intelligence.

It is also important to stress that informal procedures do obtain the kind or type of supervisors that management seems to want. The selectors know their people. Often those selected make excellent supervisors. If challenged, however, plant managements would find it difficult to defend their practices either as consistent or objective, despite the fact that, judging by the results, such selections are often impressive.

FACTORS AFFECTING SELECTION

In chapter III, a number of environmental and institutional factors which affect the process of upgrading and selecting supervisors were examined. Public policy (through EEO enforcement and pollution and environmental standards), plant location, product, and hence labor demand are the most important of the former; the nature of the work, union policies, management interest, and incentives are the most significant in the latter category; but the other factors discussed in chapter III all play a role. Of significance is the fact that, although governmental EEO enforcement agencies stress the need for objective selection criteria, these same agencies have forced companies to abandon tests and to rely on more subjective criteria. We shall return to this dilemma in the following chapters.

Whatever the environmental and institutional factors involved, it is obvious that no examination of supervisor (or other) selection procedures is complete without a thorough analysis of such factors and their impact. Management policy—itself a factor—must operate within the framework and constraints of the environmental and institutional factors, which often cannot easily, if at all, be overcome even when they are recognized. This would be true even where the upgrading and selection systems are more objective than those discussed herein. Recognition of these factors, however, gives management both a better opportunity to overcome, or at least to ameliorate, those factors which have a limiting or negative influence and to better utilize others which can be more helpful in obtaining the most desirable supervisors.

TABLE V-2

Common Supervisor Selection Criteria

First-Line Supervisors			Higher Management		
	Frequency of Response			Frequency of Response	
Criterion	Number	Percent	Criterion	Number	Percent
Ability to get along with people	8	100.0	Job knowledge, mechanical aptitude	8	100.0
Job knowledge	7	87.5	Ability to get along with people	7	87.5
Leadership	6	75.0	Intelligence, education	7	87.5
Desire, initiative	6	75.0	Leadership	6	75.0
Dependability, responsibility	6	75.0	Initiative, motivation	6	75.0
Attitude, loyalty	5	62.5			

Note: See Appendix F.
Number interviewed: First-line supervisors = 8.
Higher management = 8.

Characteristics of Supervision

Table V-3 presents a summary of the quantifiable variables that were identified by means of discriminant analysis as most significant in differentiating between hourly employees and first-line supervisors in each plant case study. (This study indicates that discriminant analysis is an area that has potential application to procedures for selecting supervisors.) Three major quantifiable variables (education, seniority, and job history), along with two nonquantifiable variables (race and sex), most frequently and accurately distinguish first-line supervisors from hourly employees.

None of these key variables are, of course, surprising. Higher management particularly emphasizes education in supervisor selection; usually, seniority either is required to learn the job or is the "default" criterion if management has adopted the criteria used for upgrading union-hourly workers; and job history is a way of looking at the employee's experience and relating that to the specifications for the supervisory function.

CONCLUSIONS

As outlined in chapter I (Figure I-3), we have utilized an organizational model to analyze the process by which hourly employees are upgraded into supervision. This model facilitated

TABLE V-3

Summary of Significant Quantifiable
Personal Data Distinguishing Foremen and Hourly Workers

Paper Manufacturer	Nonferrous Smelter	Automobile Assembly Plant	Aircraft Manufacturer
Current seniority[a]	Number of relatives and friends employed here[a]	Current seniority	Current seniority
Number of permanent jobs held at the plant	Number of organization memberships	Years of education	Years of education
Years of education	Years of education	Number of organization memberships	Number of experience areas in the plant
Number of jobs held in last five years	Number of jobs held in last five years	Number of jobs held in last five years	Age at time of plant employment
Length of last job			Length of last job
Age at time of plant employment[a]			

Electrical Products Manufacturer	Chemical Manufacturer	Food Processing Plant	Petroleum Refinery
Years of education	Current seniority	Number of organization memberships	Years of education
Number of organization memberships	Years of education	Current seniority	Current seniority
Number of dependent children		Years of education	Number of permanent jobs held at the plant
Number of relatives and friends employed here		Number of permanent jobs held at the plant[a]	
		Number of jobs held in last five years	
		Length of last job	
		Age at time of plant employment	

Note: See Appendix G.

[a] Identified as significant by 95 percent confidence intervals.

the systematic analysis and description of the actual operation or behavior of the system, the influential background factors, and the consequences of personal characteristics of the people who are upgraded into supervision. Figure V-1 summarizes the general findings of this study and fills in the facts in the general model set forth in chapter I so that the model can aid in the analysis of the upgrading systems of most internal labor markets.

The ideal of objective upgrading and selection is regularly praised by managements, union, and government officials, but relatively rarely translated into concrete efforts. That this ideal is constrained by environmental and institutional factors must be recognized. It must also be understood that different personal characteristics affect selection processes. Within any constraints, greater objectivity is both possible and desirable. The balance of this book examines two systems that are believed capable of increasing the objectivity of selection, but first, we must turn to the concept of "validity."

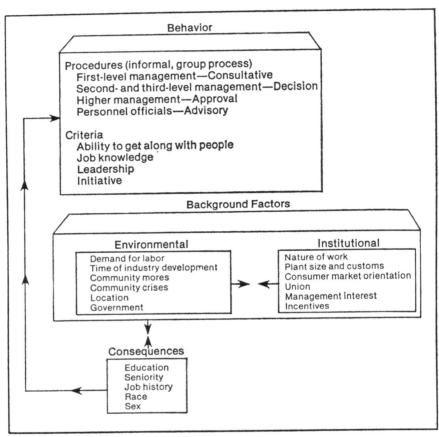

FIGURE V-1
Upgrading: Organizational Model
General Findings

PART TWO

Objective Selection

CHAPTER VI

Validation

Organizational effectiveness is dependent upon management's ability to recruit, select, and place personnel who possess the capabilities and interests necessary to achieve organizational goals. This is particularly true of such responsible jobs as the first-line supervisor's. Civil rights legislation supports this ideal, but it goes one step further and requires that the recruitment and selection techniques used to obtain prospective "successful performers" must be fair to all groups. To insure that all applicants are treated fairly in the selection process, the organization must be able to predict objectively which persons will be the most successful in a particular job. This requires managers to establish the predictive capacity of their selection methods. *Validation* is the process of demonstrating that selection procedures actually do, or do not, predict job performance. The concept of validation and the federal guidelines that have been established regarding validation are the topics of this chapter. A good grasp of the validation process and of the federal guidelines pertaining to it is necessary to understand adequately the validated selection methods to be presented in the next two chapters.

Simply stated, *validity* means that a selection instrument actually measures what it is intended to measure. Thus, "the index of validity is the extent to which a measuring instrument accomplishes the purpose for which it is intended." [1] For personnel selection, the measurement instrument, or selection tool, must measure qualities that clearly relate to performance in a specific job.

---

[1] C. Harold Stone and Floyd L. Ruch, "Selection, Interviewing, and Testing," in *American Society for Personnel Administration Handbook of Personnel and Industrial Relations*, Vol. 1, *Staffing Policies and Strategies*, ed. Dale Yoder and Herbert G. Heneman, Jr. (Washington, D.C.: Bureau of National Affairs, Inc., 1974), p. 4-135.

TWO CLASSES OF VALIDATION

Although there is no single, simple procedure for validating selection instruments, government agencies are accepting two classes of validation, "rational" and "empirical." Both classes are intended to determine whether a selection instrument (predictor) bears a relevant and significant relationship to the job to be filled. As one can discern from the following descriptions, which class an employer will pick from depends on the nature of the job and the size of his operation.

Rational Validation

Rational validation, or noncriterion-based methods of determining validity, relies heavily on human judgment of what skills a particular job demands and of what skills a particular test measures. The two methods of rational validation are those of *content validity* and *construct validity*:

> *Content validity* involves a *systematic examination of the job* and the test content to determine whether the test contains a sampling of the knowledge, skills, and behavior required for successful job performance. Thus, a typing test is a "content-valid" measure to use in hiring stenographers, although it does not cover the whole domain of stenography. A shorthand test, another content-valid measure, can help to give a more complete sampling of an applicant's stenographic skills when used with a typing test.
>
> The *construct validity* of a test refers to the extent to which the test measures a "theoretical construct" or trait. Examples of theoretical constructs are verbal ability, space visualization, and perceptual speed, to name just three aptitudes that are frequently job related. When, for example, *careful job analysis* shows that workers must read blueprints, a test of space visualization is valid as part of the employment procedure. There are many other constructs which have been shown to be job related.[2]

It is important to realize that, although not empirical, both methods, as the definitions indicate, call for careful, systematic job analysis. Under the federal government's 1978 "Uniform Guidelines on Employee Selection Procedures," rational validation, or any other method of validation, cannot involve any assumption of validity:

> Under no circumstances will the general reputation of a test or other selection procedures, its author or its publisher, or casual reports of its validity be accepted in lieu of evidence of validity.

---

[2] *Ibid.*, p. 4-125. (Emphasis added.)

Specifically ruled out are: assumptions of validity based on a procedure's name or descriptive labels; all forms of promotional literature; data bearing on the frequency of a procedure's usage; testimonial statements and credentials of sellers, users, or consultants; and other nonempirical or anecdotal accounts of selection practices or selection outcomes.

Professional supervision of selection activities is encouraged but is not a substitute for documented evidence of validity. The enforcement agencies will take into account the fact that a thorough job analysis was conducted and that careful development and use of a selection procedure in accordance with professional standards enhance the probability that the selection procedure is valid for the job.[3]

Empirical Validation

Empirical validation is criterion based; it implies

a proven, empirical relationship between test scores and performance or some other indication of success. This relationship is usually expressed in the form of a correlation coefficient. Correlations range from .00 to 1.00. The greater the relationship between the test(s) and the criterion, the higher the coefficient. In addition, the coefficient is preceded by a plus or a minus sign, which indicates the direction of the relationship; a plus correlation means a positive relationship in which high scores on the tests are related to high scores on the performance measure; a minus correlation means an inverse relationship in which high scores on the test are related to low scores on performance and vice versa.[4]

This type of validation seems to be the method most satisfactory to the government; but empirical validation *is* the method most valuable to an organization using selection tools. If, by way of criterion-based research, an organization knows that its selection tools strongly relate to future job performance, it can maximize its resource development. The organization can invest most heavily in those who have a greater probability of job success; this is the true value of validated selection tools.

For empirically validating selection tools, there are two methods: *concurrent validation* and *predictive validation*. With concurrent validation, present employees are tested, and the

---

[3] "Uniform Guidelines on Employee Selection Procedures," *Daily Labor Report*, August 25, 1978, Special Supplement, p. 10.

[4] William C. Byham and Morton E. Spitzer, *The Law and Personnel Testing* (New York: American Management Association, Inc., 1971), p. 116.

results are statistically analyzed to determine if there are significant differences between the scores of good job performers and those of poor job performers. If there are significant differences, then the test is valid and can be used with job applicants. With predictive validation, "in its purest form, all applicants are tested prior to employment, but their scores are not used in making the employment decision. Later, these scores are correlated with a measure of training or job success to see whether those with high scores do substantially better than those with low scores." [5]

Although both methods, when applied correctly, yield results that are acceptable under the 1978 federal guidelines, neither is without its disadvantages. For example, concurrent validation depends on the assumptions that present employees are similar to applicants being recruited, "that knowledge or interest measured by the test is not acquired on the job," and that the difference between a good applicant and a poor applicant is the same as that between a really good job performer and a really poor job performer.[6] The disadvantages of predictive validation involve time and cost; one must assume that the nature of the employees and the nature of the job are inalterable during the period which must elapse before the criterion of success is obtainable, that the applicant population will not change during that period, and that the organization can afford this delay and the ongoing hiring of poorer applicants.[7]

VALIDATION ISSUES

All validation studies suffer in one way or another from various measurement problems. The first of these is the numbers problem; proper statistical validation requires a rather large number of employees, a problem for the small company. The criterion problem, the difficulty of clearly specifying what determines managerial effectiveness, also plagues validity studies. So-called objective standards, when closely examined, often can be demonstrated to be neither objective nor relevant. Salary, a frequently used criterion, may be only a function of prejudice, time, or some other subjective evaluation. The criterion problem may be

---

[5] Stone and Ruch, "Selection," p. 4-125.

[6] Byham and Spitzer, *The Law*, pp. 116-17.

[7] *Ibid.*, pp. 117-18.

major because the job criterion plays a significant role in defining the validity of assessment and, at the same time, is what assessment tries to predict. Therefore, if the criterion is not delineated as objectively and as accurately as possible, assessment procedures may be valueless, no matter how good they are. Other issues that one must face, or at least be aware of, when conducting validation studies are differential validity, reliability, objectivity, and standardization.

Differential Validity

One question that is always on the minds of those who construct tests is, For what groups of people may the test be used? It is relatively obvious that a test with instructions, stories, and questions stated in French would not be suitable for a group that did not know French, especially if there were no intent to determine the group's fluency in French. The test's applicability becomes more uncertain when the group to be tested is of a different membership (race, sex, ethnic, etc.) than the group for which the test was designed, even though the groups use the same basic language. If this situation does occur, then noticeable variances in test scores among the different groups might be explained by a group's ability to understand the questions or concepts used in the test. For example, this type of situation became an issue when tests were used for people of widely varying ages. The problem was dealt with by determining and making adjustments in the raw test scores for people of certain ages.

In the 1950s and 1960s, similar questions were raised about the applicability of tests for people from different ethnic and racial groups. Specifically, the subject became an issue when it was established that blacks usually score lower on tests than whites score.[8] Many psychologists believed that these differences were caused by environmental effects rather than innate differences.[9]

The notion that tests may not be equally valid for members of different ethnic and racial groups and result in unfair discrimination has generated considerable controversy over the use of tests in the selection process. Research as late as 1973, however, has cast serious doubt on the existence of differential

---

[8] James J. Kirkpatrick et al., *Testing and Fair Employment* (New York: New York University Press, 1968), p. 5.

[9] *Ibid.*

validity as a substantive phenomenon.[10] Nevertheless, the 1978 federal guidelines incorporate the concept of differential validity within the definition of test unfairness; thus, differential validity remains an important legal issue to consider.

Reliability

Essentially, reliability refers to the ability of a selection instrument to produce consistent results. That is, a reliable test is one on which applicants should be able to achieve the same relative scores each time they are tested. To be valid, a selection device must be reliable. By itself, however, reliability does not guarantee validity.

Objectivity

For a selection instrument to be reliable, it must pass the test of objectivity. This means that the measurement device must be capable of producing results that can be scored on an objective basis. Two or more persons must score an applicant's responses in a manner that achieves the same results.

Standardization

In order that the scores of job applicants can be compared in a meaningful way, a selection instrument must be standardized. This requires that "norms" be established for each instrument. Norms are derived by administering the selection instrument to persons successfully employed in the job under study. For example, to arrive at standards for a patterned interview used to select factory foremen in a particular plant, the patterned interview would be administered to persons employed as factory foremen in this specific plant.

FEDERAL GUIDELINES AND VALIDATION

Besides these various issues to be considered when a selection instrument is being validated is the government's interest in selection procedures, an interest manifest in laws and written and rewritten guidelines. On December 30, 1977, a set of uniform federal guidelines for employee selection procedures was proposed by the Carter Administration. A final draft of these

---

[10] Frank L. Schmidt, John G. Berner, and John G. Hunter, "Racial Differences in Validity of Employment Tests: Reality or Illusion?" *Journal of Applied Psychology*, Vol. 58 (August 1973), pp. 5-9.

guidelines was published on August 25, 1978, after intense debate over certain sections of the document. These long-awaited guidelines do provide employers with a single set of principles covering the use of tests and other selection procedures; but these principles are still not clear of controversy, and much litigation appears likely. It is clear at least that employers are expected to use procedures that are valid and to conduct validation studies if evidence exists that their procedures have an adverse impact on minorities. These guidelines also spell out the general standards for validity studies. Under the validation standards, "users may rely upon criterion-related validity studies, content validity studies, or construct validity studies." [11]

The 1978 "Uniform Guidelines on Employee Selection Procedures" represents an agreement on the part of four federal agencies, the Department of Justice, the Equal Employment Opportunity Commission, the Department of Labor, and the U.S. Civil Service Commission, to reconcile their differences regarding the use of tests and other selection procedures in employment decisions. The result of this reconciliation is to eliminate two different sets of guidelines which have been in effect since November 1976: the "Guidelines on Employee Selection Procedures" of the Equal Employment Opportunity Commission,[12] and the "Federal Executive Agency Guidelines on Employee Selection Procedures." [13] Chapter X of our study deals in general with employee selection and the law and in particular with the legal implications of these new guidelines.

VALIDATION IN PRACTICE

In summary, there are two major classes of validation, and each class has two methods. The two classes are empirical and rational. The predictive and concurrent methods fall within the empirical (criterion based) class, while the content and construct methods fall within the rational (noncriterion based). The EEOC requires the use of empirical validation methods where practical. In addition to proving the validity of selection instruments by one or more of the above methods, employers have three additional tests to apply to their selection tools— reliability, objectivity, and standardization.

---

[11] "Uniform Guidelines," p. 9.

[12] 29 *Code of Federal Regulations (C.F.R.)* § 1607 (1970).

[13] *Federal Register* 41, November 23, 1976, p. 51734.

Although the above summarized methods and specifications of validation of selection devices *should* be used by employers, apparently few organizations *actually* do validation research. "The method of validating . . . (if done at all) is employed after many of the personnel decisions have been made and is, in part, more of . . . historical interest." [14] In addition, "any survey of prevailing managerial assessment practices will show that they are largely intuitive, prone to wide margins of error, and based largely on the idea that the principal factor to be assessed is past experience." [15]

---

[14] D. L. Hardesty and W. S. Jones, "Characteristics of Judged High-Potential Management Personnel—The Operations of an Industrial Assessment Center," *Personnel Psychology*, Vol. 21 (Spring 1968), pp. 86-87.

[15] Felix M. Lopez, *The Making of a Manager* (New York: American Management Association, Inc., 1970), p. 145.

CHAPTER VII

The Assessment Center Method

The combination of management's desire to select managers of high quality and the federal government's policy of demanding objective proof of nondiscriminatory selection has generated substantial interest in the assessment center method. In 1969, only twelve American organizations employed this method; by 1977, over one thousand organizations worldwide were using it.[1] Even prior to 1973, the increased use of the assessment center method and of other "broad band" selection techniques had been called one of the major developments in the selection field in the years to come.[2] Interest in the assessment center method has grown not only because of such acclaim but also because the method has demonstrated its superiority over traditional selection techniques in the organizations which have used it.

DEFINITION

The assessment center method is holistic; it engages almost totally the personalities of candidates for upgrading and provides an analytical and evaluative structure whereby a number of assessors can observe the candidates and can combine several predictors to form an overall rating of potential for each candidate. Based on the well-established principle that early behavior tends to persist, the method consists of a variety of standardized tests and a system of simulations of actual work-related problems and complex situations that elicit behavior clearly related to success in a supervisory position. In experi-

---

[1] William C. Byham, "Application of the Assessment Center Method," in *Applying the Assessment Center Method,* ed. Joseph L. Moses and William C. Byham (New York: Pergamon Press, 1977), pp. 31, 33. See Appendix H for a partial listing of organizations and governments that use the assessment center method.

[2] Douglas W. Bray and Joseph L. Moses, "Personnel Selection," in *Annual Review of Psychology,* ed. Paul H. Mussen and Mark R. Rosenzweig (Palo Alto: Annual Reviews, Inc., 1972), p. 569.

mental psychology's terms, assessment itself links two or more instances of behavior: the assessment behavior is the independent variable; the criterion (job) behavior is the dependent variable; and the link between the two is the basis for the validation of assessment (see chapter VI). If designed and applied properly, an assessment center program facilitates this linkage and strengthens the validity of the assessment process.

Any definition of the assessment center method must allow for the adaptability that is one of the method's major strengths. The individual characteristics of the many assessment center programs in operation vary greatly; time required, cost, contents, staffing, administration, and selection of candidates differ because they depend upon the company's objective in assessment, the dimensions to be assessed, and the employee population. Underlying those variations, however, are these requirements:

—Multiple assessment techniques must be used. At least one of these techniques must be a simulation.

  A simulation is an exercise or technique designed to elicit behaviors related to dimensions of performance on the job by requiring the participant to respond behaviorally to situational stimuli. The stimuli present in a simulation parallel or resemble stimuli in the work situation. Examples of simulations include group exercises, in-basket exercises, and fact-finding exercises.

—Multiple assessors must be used. These assessors must receive training prior to participating in a center.

—Judgments resulting in an outcome (i.e., recommendation for promotion, specific training or development) must be based on pooling information from assessors and techniques.

—An overall evaluation of behavior must be made by the assessors at a separate time from observation of behavior.

—Simulation exercises are used. These exercises are developed to tap a variety of predetermined behaviors and have been pretested prior to use to insure that the techniques provide reliable, objective, and relevant behavioral information for the organization in question.

—The dimensions, attributes, characteristics, or qualities evaluated by the assessment center are determined by an analysis of relevant job behaviors.

—The techniques used in the assessment center are designed to provide information which is used in evaluating the dimensions, attributes, or qualities previously determined.[3]

---

[3] Joseph L. Moses and William C. Byham, eds., *Applying the Assessment Center Method* (New York: Pergamon Press, 1977), pp. 304-5. These require-

History

The assessment center method did not spring up in full bloom. From 1911 to the mid-1950s, the development of assessment methodology was primarily in the hands of the German, Japanese, British, and American military. In 1956, using the multiple assessment techniques developed by the military, such as leaderless group discussions and "real life" or situational exercises, American Telephone and Telegraph (AT&T) launched its Management Progress Study to assess the career potentials of employees who either had been recruited as management trainees or had moved up to management positions. AT&T followed this "first" in industrial research with a "first" in industrial practice. In 1958, Michigan Bell Telephone Company initiated its Personnel Assessment Program, which uses multiple assessment techniques to select the potentially successful from nonmanagement or craft personnel in line for promotion to first-level management. Other large organizations were quick to follow Michigan Bell's lead: Standard Oil of Ohio; International Business Machines; General Electric; and Sears, Roebuck and Company; among others.[4] Today, as mentioned before, hundreds of other organizations employ the assessment center method; consequently, it has been refined and extended, and many of its aspects subjected to innovation so that any company, regardless of size, can use the assessment center method for such varied purposes as placement, early identification of talent, development, training, career "tracking," and identification of target groups for upgrading, such as minorities or women.

History and Our Examination of the Assessment Center Method

Of all the important years in the assessment center method's history and of all the organizations involved in the method's development, 1973 and AT&T assume special significance for our study. The federal government tacitly approved the assessment center method as a nondiscriminatory selection device when

ments were endorsed by the Third International Congress on the Assessment Center Method, Quebec, Canada, May 1975.

[4] The preceding history is summarized from Barry M. Cohen, Joseph L. Moses, and William C. Byham, *The Validity of Assessment Centers: A Literature Review* (Pittsburgh: Development Dimensions, Inc., 1974), pp. 3-8; and James R. Huck, "Determinants of Assessment Center Ratings for White and Black Females and the Relationship of These Dimensions to Subsequent Performance Effectiveness" (Ph.D. diss., Wayne State University, 1974), pp. 1-4.

the January 1973 Consent Decree was issued to AT&T.[5] The "affected class" included women hired into management positions between July 1965 and December 1971 and not placed in the company's "fast track" development program. An assessment center program was used to determine the third-level management potential of those women in the affected class who elected to attend. Ninety-two percent (1,701) of the eligible women chose to attend the center; 42 percent of those assessed were designated as having high third-level potential and received immediate salary increases, and their names were placed on a third-level promotion list.[6] By identifying women and minorities with high potential, breaking down the usual barriers to these groups' mobility among departments and jobs, and serving to encourage candidates through personal feedback, the assessment center method is assisting AT&T in changing the traditional beliefs about women and minorities as managers.

Because we are concerned here with *validated, objective* procedures for selecting supervisory personnel, we have used Michigan Bell's Personnel Assessment Program as a touchstone in the next section as we present both a general and particular picture of the assessment center method.

THE ANATOMY OF AN ASSESSMENT CENTER PROGRAM

With almost one million employees, the Bell System is immense and complex; in 1977, there were over nineteen thousand "accessions to, and within, management" in the system.[7] Obviously, the costs of a faulty system for selecting supervisors would be high. Because it wanted to discover the qualities that distinguish effective managers from ineffective managers and to adjust its selection system to insure that a higher proportion of those

---

[5] *Equal Employment Opportunity Commission et al.* v. *American Telephone and Telegraph Company et al.*, 365 F.Supp. 1105 (E.D. Pa. 1973).

[6] David F. Hoyle, "AT&T Completes Assessment of Nearly 1,700 Women Under Consent Agreement," *Assessment & Development*, Vol. 2 (January 1975), pp. 4-5; and David Robison, "AT&T Women Employees Making Faster Strides into Middle Management," *World of Work Report*, Vol. 3 (January 1978), p. 6.

[7] David F. Hoyle, AT&T manager—Assessment and Selection, to the author, June 6, 1978. Unless otherwise noted, the information here about the Michigan Bell Personnel Assessment Program and about AT&T is based on interviews and correspondence with David F. Hoyle and Michigan Bell assessment center personnel in March 1975 and from May to June 1978.

promoted would be effective, Michigan Bell turned to the assessment center method used by the Management Progress Study, modified the method, and instituted the first industrially applied assessment center program, the Personnel Assessment Program.

An employee's participation in the PAP depends upon nomination by his supervisor or by himself. Once assembled from the company's departments, the block of candidates is divided into groups of twelve. For two days, six assessors administer tests and questionnaires and conduct interviews and three situational exercises. In Michigan Bell's program and in most other operational centers, the projective techniques, attitudinal questionnaires, and much of the paper-and-pencil tests of the Management Progress Study have been eliminated because their administration requires a psychologist and because Michigan Bell, like many other companies that have established assessment center programs, prefers to use its own management personnel for staffing.

The absence of a psychologist and the elimination of the projective tests, however, do not mean that the techniques used are not standardized. The assessors are given a thorough and consistent understanding of the assessment exercises and of the behavior they are intended to evoke. Furthermore, the qualities to be measured by the assessment center method must meet four important criteria. First, the quality tested should be an important managerial attribute. Second, it should be simple enough to define in behavioral terms. Third, it should be observable enough in the exercises so that reasonably accurate predictions about a candidate's behavior may be made. Finally, the characteristic should remain stable over time so that future predictions are worthwhile and valid.

The PAP examines eighteen variables (see Table VII-1) drawn from the Management Progress Study. For the study, twenty-five variables had been selected from three sources: management and psychological literature outlining qualities important to managerial success, variables "proposed by several behavioral scientists outside the Bell System," and senior personnel executives within the company.[8] Of course, among assessment center programs, the number of variables may range from ten to

---

[8] Douglas W. Bray, Richard J. Campbell, and Donald L. Grant, *Formative Years in Business: A Long-Term AT&T Study of Managerial Lives* (New York: John Wiley & Sons, 1974), p. 18.

TABLE VII-1
The PAP Variables

---

1. *Energy*—To what extent can this individual maintain a continuous high level of work activity?

2. *Resistance to stress*—To what extent will this individual's work performance stand up in the face of unusual pressures?

3. *Inner work standards*—To what extent will this individual want to do a good job, even if he could get by with doing a less acceptable job?

4. *Self-objectivity*—To what extent does this individual realize his own assets and liabilities?

5. *Managerial identification*—To what extent has this individual incorporated (or is likely to incorporate) values such as service, friendliness, justice of company position on earnings, rates, wages, etc.?

6. *Forcefulness*—To what extent does this individual make an early impact on others?

7. *Likeability*—To what extent does this individual make a likeable impact on the staff?

8. *Range of interest*—To what extent is this individual interested in a variety of fields of activity such as science, politics, sports, music, art, etc.?

9. *Scholastic aptitude*—To what extent does this individual compare to other individuals in his ability to learn new things?

10. *Awareness of social environment*—To what extent can this individual perceive subtle cues in the behavior of others toward him?

11. *Behavior flexibility*—To what extent can this individual, when motivated, modify his behavior to reach a goal?

12. *Leadership*—How effectively can this individual lead a group to accomplish a task without arousing hostility?

13. *Need for superior approval*—To what extent does this individual have a need to have his behavior approved of by those he views as his superiors?

14. *Need for peer approval*—To what extent does this individual have a need to have his behavior approved of by those he views as his peers?

15. *Organizing and planning*—To what extent can this individual effectively organize and plan his work?

16. *Decision making*—To what extent can this individual make decisions of high quality, and how likely is he to make decisions when required?

17. *Oral communications skill*—To what extent can this individual effectively present an oral report to a small conference group?

18. *Written communications skill*—To what extent can this individual effectively express his ideas in writing?

Source: "AT&T Personnel Assessment Program Administrator's Guide" (New York, 1974).

thirty-eight.[9] *All* variables indicating management potential cannot, however, be measured by the assessment center method. Important traits such as loyalty, integrity, and ethics can be observed only in the field.

---

[9] Donald W. MacKinnon, *An Overview of Assessment Centers*, Center for Creative Leadership, Technical Report No. 1 (Greensboro, N.C.: Center for Creative Leadership, 1975), p. 8.

After the two days of exercises, the assessors, usually second-level managers, gather to evaluate each candidate, each evaluation requiring two to three hours. The results of each assessment technique are examined; each assessor, using a one-to-five scale, rates the candidate on every variable and then gives the candidate an Overall Assessment Rating (see Table VII-2). This entire process is characterized by the staff members' careful discussion of each variable rating and of the Overall Assessment Rating (OAR); although agreement is not required, the staff members are permitted to change their ratings in the course of the discussion. The result of the assessment process is the central administrator's narrative report, outlining the decision and developmental recommendations of the assessment staff. Finally, a conference is held between the candidate, his superior, and an assessment center staff member to discuss the candidate's performance in the program.

The conference for feedback is one of the more delicate aspects of the PAP and all assessment center programs. Like the PAP, some programs even make such feedback optional for the can-

TABLE VII-2

Definitions of Overall Assessment Ratings

---

5   Above the Norm

Overall performance at the Assessment Center was rated above the norm by the staff. The assessee demonstrated management skills that exceeded first-level supervision requirements.

4   Met the Norm

Overall performance at the Assessment Center was rated at the norm by the staff. The assessee demonstrated management skills that met first-level supervision requirements.

3   Moderate

Overall performance at the Assessment Center was rated below the norm by the staff. The assessee demonstrated strengths in some management skills that indicated moderate potential to meet first-level supervision requirements.

2   Limited

Overall performance at the Assessment Center was rated below the norm by the staff. The assessee demonstrated weaknesses in management skills that indicated limited potential to meet first-level supervision requirements.

1   Low

Overall performance at the Assessment Center was rated below the norm by the staff. The assessee demonstrated weaknesses in management skills that indicated significantly limited potential to meet first-level supervision requirements.

Source: James R. Huck and Douglas W. Bray, "Management Assessment Center Evaluations and Subsequent Job Performance of White and Black Females," *Personnel Psychology,* Vol. 29 (1976), p. 16. Reprinted by permission of Personnel Psychology, Inc.

didates. When the candidate chooses to have the conference, the PAP assessor's primary task is to give the candidate a clear understanding of how the staff viewed his performance; but, the assessor will also present as much of the assessment as possible in a developmental framework. With higher level assessment programs in AT&T, and in most other organizations' programs, the developmental framework takes on greater importance.

Throughout the program, right down to the feedback conference, the assessment techniques, the staff, and the candidates are constantly and dynamically interacting. In a sense, the exercises, the staff, and the candidates constitute the anatomy of an assessment center program.

The Exercises

There is nothing mysterious about the assessment process. Managers observe and evaluate the behavior of their subordinates every day. By manipulating circumstances and situations, the assessment center method intensifies this informal procedure and helps managers who act as assessors by giving them a structured method of observation and a rigorous analytical technique.

The assessment techniques used in the PAP include the following:

Personal Interview. A one-and-one-half-hour interview is conducted by an assessor with each assessee. It is directed toward obtaining insights into the individual's personal development up to that time, his work objectives, attitudes toward company policies, range of interest, and motivation. (In other companies, interviews vary in terms of structure, standardization of interpretation, and the general climate in which they are conducted.)

In-Basket. The candidate is presented with a set of materials that a Bell System manager might expect to find in his In-Basket. The twenty-five items encompass many things, from production reports to letters from customers. The subject is provided with the necessary material to complete the exercise, such as a copy of the union contract, management guide, organization chart, and stationery. Three hours are allotted to take appropriate action on the items by writing letters and memos, delegating, and so on. Following completion, each candidate undergoes an interview with an assessor to determine his approach to the task, reasons for taking actions, and opinions of peers and supervisors.

No prior experience is necessary, but an individual's ability to establish priorities, make decisions, anticipate the consequences of those decisions, organize the work load through proper delegation, and communicate both within and without the organization are assessed. The assessor observes whether the assessee is systematic, spots connections between related problems, and makes use of the staff or whether he gets bogged down in detail and ignores important matters. (The In-Basket materials are tailored to meet the needs of an individual company and position, but the basic structure is consistent.)

Small Business Problem. This is a manufacturing game wherein the participants assume the roles of partners in an enterprise manufacturing toys for handicapped children. This cooperative venture in an unstructured environment requires participants to buy parts and sell finished products under changing market conditions, to maintain inventories, and to manufacture toys.

Management games, as used in Michigan and other companies, usually require participants to solve problems, either cooperatively or competitively. Topics include the problem described above, stock market tasks, or merger negotiations. The games should be geared to the level of the job concerned. They elicit leadership, organizational abilities, interpersonal skills, and sometimes reactions under stress.

Promotion Problem. This is an assigned-role, leaderless group discussion centering on a management personnel function. The participants assume the roles of managers, each having a supervisor capable of promotion reporting to them. During the oral presentation phase of the problem, each assessee has five minutes to present a description of his supervisor. The group then discusses the assets and liabilities of each hypothetical supervisor, and it tries to reach a group decision on the relative promotability of each. Compared to the Small Business Problem, this exercise is more structured and involves more competition.

The purpose of the leaderless group discussion is to examine the interpersonal skills of the assessees. No formal organizational roles are involved, nor is the authority which usually accompanies the title. Some individuals take control of the situation and lead the group, while others just sit, fearful of entering the discussion. A definite advantage of this exercise is that it provides an opportunity to view directly how well an individual interacts with others. As the assessees interact, the assessors (usually three present) describe and evaluate their group influence, verbal skills, flexibility, and interpersonal relations.

Q-Sort. Here the candidate is presented with seventy personal statements and asked to sort the statements into seven categories ranging from those which best describe himself to those which least describe himself. The Q-Sort provides more data regarding self-objectivity.

Paper-and-Pencil Test. This includes three separate tests. The School and College Ability Test (SCAT) is designed to measure general mental ability or learning ability. The General Information Test (GIT) provides a measure of the assessee's range of interest. The third item is a short autobiographical letter written by the candidate; it describes his job and how it relates to overall company operation. This essay is scored on its unity and thesis, coherence, idea development, sentence structure, diction, style, and general effectiveness.

Personal History Questionnaire. The questionnaire requests biographical information, such as educational background, previous work experience, and so on.[10]

Table VII-3 provides an overview of the variables that some of the techniques are designed to tap.

Obviously, an assessment center program's success is partially dependent upon the proper selection of techniques. In selecting the techniques, we must constantly ask, What do exercises in an assessment center program measure? Some say that a center measures *actual* management skills by forcing a candidate to demonstrate decisiveness, analytical thinking, interpersonal skills, etc. Others argue that the centers do not measure *specific* on-the-job behavior, but place the candidate in a situation in which some managerial characteristics will have to be displayed to complete the task. In 1965, two investigators testing the hypothesis that centers mainly measure skill and sensitivity in interpersonal relations found that "the individual's interpersonal skills and underlying psychological characteristics play a major role in the final assessment center rating." [11] Drawing on factor analyses and comparing the dimensions targeted by different assessment center programs, one researcher states, "if one were to ask what is measured by the assessment center method in the most simple and general sense, the answer would have to describe in some fashion the ability to express thoughts to others and to influence others in their course of action." [12]

Among the techniques, there is therefore a relative importance that can be measured by the extent to which each technique most consistently elicits behavior demonstrating those basic managerial dimensions. Most agree that, whatever is being measured at the center, the In-Basket and group exercises are *where* it is

---

[10] Huck, "Determinants of Assessment Center Ratings," pp. 36-39; and David F. Hoyle, coordinator, AT&T Management Assessment Program, interview at Woodhaven, Michigan, March 1975.

[11] John E. Wilson and Walter A. Tatge, "Assessment Centers—Further Assessment Needed?" *Personnel Journal*, Vol. 52 (March 1973), p. 177.

[12] Thomas E. Standing, "Assessment and Management Selection," in *Applying the Assessment Center Method*, ed. Joseph L. Moses and William C. Byham (New York: Pergamon Press, 1977), p. 194.

TABLE VII-3

*Sources of Evidence for Assessment Variables
by Assessment Techniques*

Variable	Personal Interview	Promotion Problem	In-Basket	Small Business	Tests
Energy	X	X	X	X	
Resistance to Stress	X	X	X	X	
Inner Work Standards	X	X	X	X	
Self-Objectivity		X	X	X	X
Managerial Identification	X				
Forcefulness	X	X	X	X	
Likeability	X	X	X	X	
Range of Interest	X				X
Scholastic Aptitude					X
Awareness of Social Environment		X	X	X	
Behavior Flexibility		X		X	
Leadership		X		X	
Need for Superior Approval	X		X		
Need for Peer Approval		X		X	
Organizing and Planning			X		
Decision Making			X		
Oral Communications Skill		X			
Written Communications Skill					X

Source: "AT&T Personnel Assessment Program Administrator's Guide" (New York, 1974).

measured. Analysis of the Management Progress Study shows that:

> Judgments of administrative skills are determined most strongly by performance on the In-Basket test.
>
> Evaluations of interpersonal skills depend most heavily on behavior as seen in the group exercises.
>
> Ratings of intellectual ability are, of course, quite directly influenced by scores on paper-and-pencil ability tests.
>
> Judgments of stability of performance are most dependent . . . on performance in the simulations.
>
> Work motivation is seen most clearly in the projective tests and the interview, with additional contributions from the simulations.
>
> Career orientation is strongly apparent in the projective tests and interview reports; it is in connection with this factor that person-

ality questionnaires make their only important contribution to assessment judgments.

Judgments of dependency on others rest most heavily on the projective test reports.[13]

From these observations, it is clear that the In-Basket and other situational exercises demand much of a candidate's ability to make decisions, to communicate clearly in writing and speaking, and to influence others' actions.

What adds to the strength of these exercises is that the demands that they do make on a candidate can be adjusted to reflect the real demands of a specific job or job level. For first-line selection, the whom-to-promote leaderless group discussion in Michigan Bell's program is an appropriate exercise because the decision to be made is relatively simple and straightforward. If the assessees were upper-level management candidates, a more complex variation of this exercise could be employed. Many jobs have a unique and highly important aspect, and special exercises can be developed to simulate these aspects.

[J. C.] Penney has developed an effective exercise called the Irate Customer Phone Call. During dinner on the first night of the program, the candidates are told that they are to play the role of a manager during the evening and that they may receive a phone call between 8:00 and 10:00 that night. This phone call is from an assessor playing an irate customer who makes several unreasonable demands on the candidate, after thoroughly convincing him of how upset he is about a service matter. The candidate's ability to handle this situation is evaluated along several dimensions, such as tact under stress.

The Peace Corps puts individual volunteers into a mock community development meeting with host nationals. The volunteer has been briefed in writing by the previous Peace Corps volunteer for the area, who has stated that the most important thing for the community is to bring in fresh, uncontaminated water from the nearby mountain. The purpose of this exercise is to determine the extent to which the new man will follow and push the ideas of the previous volunteer and the extent to which he will listen to the host nationals and form his own judgments.

At the meeting, the host nationals propose their own pet (and conflicting) projects. Depending on the characteristics of the people of the particular country being simulated, they ignore the volunteer's proposals, demonstrate impatience, pretend lack of understanding, exhibit hostility, and so on. They demand that the volunteer raise money or redesign plans, and a national might try to

---

[13] Bray, Campbell, and Grant, *Formative Years*, pp. 79-80.

win over the volunteer to his own schemes through subtle persuasion or flattery.[14]

Despite our emphasis on the situational exercises, however, the strength of the overall rating of a candidate's performance at the assessment center lies in the holistic character of the assessment center method's design. When skillfully applied, the exercises (and, thus, the overall rating) are more than the sum of their parts. That skillful application depends, however, upon the staff and its training.

The Staff

"Probably the most important single factor to the success of an Assessment Center is a corps of highly-qualified and trained assessors." [15] Staffing presents several hard decisions—hard because of the controversy of psychologist vs. line manager as assessor, because of the need to consider well-calculated, preconceived purposes for the program, because of the flux that may be created in a company's managerial manpower, and because of staffing's importance to the program's success.

Whether to use psychologists or line managers as assessors has not been definitively resolved. Are psychologists, because of their superior training in observation of behavior, better assessors than managers are? The limited research available indicates that they are not. The results of two IBM researchers' studies indicate "that the selection of evaluators for . . . assessment need not be based on whether they have completed an extensive training program or have professional experience in personnel assessment." [16] Also, "the comparison between professional and nonprofessional evaluators indicated that their ratings are about equivalent for a specific group of participants being assessed." [17] Psychologists may, however, be of value in areas other than participation as assessors; Byham lists the following:

---

[14] William C. Byham, "Assessment Centers for Spotting Future Managers," *Harvard Business Review*, Vol. 48 (July 1970), p. 158.

[15] Frank Di Costanzo and Thomas Andretta, "The Supervisory Assessment Center in the Internal Revenue Service," *Training and Development Journal*, Vol. 24 (September 1970), p. 13.

[16] John M. Greenwood and Walter J. McNamara, "Interrater Reliability in Situational Tests," *Journal of Applied Psychology*, Vol. 51 (April 1967), p. 105.

[17] *Ibid.*, pp. 105-6.

Aiding managers to identify kinds of behavior that are critical to success.

Developing or selecting assessment center exercises to bring out these kinds of behavior in the candidates.

Training assessors.

Administering pilot programs.

Reviewing, critiquing, and improving the program.

Researching the program's effectiveness.[18]

The nearly universal use of line managers as assessors, however, is probably the most important reason for management's and assessees' ready acceptance and approval of the assessment center method.

As assessors, line managers are the ones most familiar with the jobs for which the candidates are being assessed, and, so, are more able to judge a candidate's aptitude for the position. Assessors can be chosen for their job background to coincide with the program's purpose. For example, when broad managerial aptitudes are being assessed, assessors can be drawn from many different areas in the company to broaden the assessment center staff's perspectives. Management participation has other benefits, too. Participation as an assessor is claimed to be a developmental experience similar to a management-training program. Another advantage of exposing line managers to the assessment center method is that it increases their familiarity with the program and assures that the most effective use of the results will be made. Too often, when presented with traditional paper-and-pencil test results, a manager tends either to overrely or underrely on them. Managers have difficulty in determining the correct emphasis to place on tests because they are not acquainted with the test, the tester, or the intent of the program. There is minimal chance of this occurring with the assessment center method if the manager has participated in its operation.

Assessors are usually chosen by their superiors with the help of the program director. This practice, though, has its dangers, for once a program has passed from its experimental to operational stage, standards may fall, and management may be tempted to send "cooperative" assessors. The director has two ways to avoid this problem; he can weed out unacceptable assessors during the training program, or he may advocate the establishment of a pool of assessors to make it easy to bypass unfit assessors.[19]

---

[18] Byham, "Assessment Centers," p. 159.

[19] *Ibid.*, p. 156.

Theoretically, good managers should need little training to become assessors; the observational and evaluative skills required of an assessor parallel those required of a manager. But the skills are only parallel; those required of an assessor must be keener and based on the philosophy behind the assessment center method. In fact, "companies [have] reported marked improvements in the reliability of supervisory ratings after the supervisors had been trained to work as assessors." [20] Even good managers must be instructed in the "art of observation" lest they focus on superficial characteristics during the assessment exercises; they must have a thorough understanding of those exercises and the behavior which they are intended to evoke; and they must know to record specific examples of behavior instead of broad statements.

The usual AT&T center for the assessment of first-level potential has eight staff members: a district-level director, six second-level assessors, and a first- or second-level administrative coordinator. Assignment to the center is full-time, each assessor serving a six-month term and the program director serving a one-year term. The director is appointed two months prior to the starting date to allow enough time for him to be trained by the personnel research staff. This director participates in the selection of assessors, who then receive three weeks of training.

An alternative to the PAP's method of staffing is to establish a pool of trained assessors and require them to serve once or twice a year. Both practices have advantages and disadvantages. Longer assignment periods guarantee a broad and in-depth experience, and fewer managers, in any given year, are kept away from their jobs. Briefer appointments, however, enable the recruitment of better men, generate greater enthusiasm and effort, and allow more managers to reap the benefits of being assessors.

Assessor training has not been standardized among the operational assessment programs. AT&T spends weeks training assessors, whereas some other companies spend only a certain number of hours. During the training program, the managers "may experience assessment as an assessee, watch videotapes of assessment exercises, study assessment manuals and forms, serve as an observer of an assessment center making ratings as non-

---

[20] *Ibid.*, p. 157.

voting members of the staff, and have their assessment judgments checked by an experienced assessor." [21] Whatever the training methods, they will force the staff-to-be to focus (1) on absorbing the organization's purposes in assessment, (2) on understanding the variables selected and the dynamics of the techniques selected to evoke behavior that will reveal a candidate's lack or possession of those variables, (3) on properly administering the exercises, and (4) on using the rating scale and deriving from it the overall rating.

The Candidates

If, as with most assessment center programs, a supervisor has nominated a candidate on the basis of job performance and potential for promotion, then one of the method's main objectives —to avoid subjective, nonstandardized supervisory judgment in promotion decisions—has been violated. Michigan Bell has sidestepped this philosophical inconsistency by permitting self-nomination. Other solutions would be to permit nominations by peers or to establish automatic assessment of personnel who have reached a certain level or served a certain number of years with the organization.

But who the candidates are depends, of course, on the purpose and level of the program. At Michigan Bell, the candidates for first-level supervisory positions are drawn from the various company departments and are typically not college educated. AT&T has applied a one-day assessment center program to new employment; and even though the process is large and expensive, the company feels that the results justify its continuance. Middle-management programs are becoming increasingly popular, but higher level programs are still in their infancy because of the sensitivity of promotions at this level. For almost two decades, though, Southern Bell and South Central Bell have conducted a program for assessing upper management potential; in 1978, this program was revised for trial throughout the Bell System. In the public sector, the Office of Management and the Budget and the Civil Service Commission have also applied the method to higher management levels. [22]

Another factor determining who the participants will be is a company's need to meet government agencies', especially the

---

[21] MacKinnon, *An Overview*, p. 9.

[22] Byham, "Application of the Assessment Center Method," p. 41.

Equal Employment Opportunity Commission's, requirements for employment and promotion procedures. For example, because of its 1973 Consent Decree, AT&T has concentrated on enrolling women and minorities in its assessment center programs. Though not necessarily because of EEOC requirements, other companies, too, have used assessment center programs to determine supervisory potential among those in disadvantaged groups.

Starting an Assessment Center Program

Implicit in our discussion so far have been the questions to be asked, the issues to be understood, and the caveats to be considered as an assessment center program is begun. Those implicit "constants" or issues are what unify a program: the program's purposes, the concern with validity at every step, the concern with the program's impact, etc. The incremental list of constants that follows is not a definitive "how-to-start-a-program" handbook; indeed, two issues, validity and impact, have been reserved for further discussion in this chapter. Rather, the list is a final touch to the more general aspects of the description that we set out to give of the assessment center method's anatomy.

The first step in starting an assessment center program is to determine its goals and objectives. Will the primary goal be selection or development or a combination? Who will be the candidates, and who will be the assessors? How will the final reports be used? Another question to be asked at this step is, What overall impact will this program have on the company's structure, its finances, and its employees?

The second step is to define the dimensions to be assessed. This is done by way of a thorough job analysis to determine the major job elements. A list of dimensions for a managerial job is not a list of the characteristics of the perfect manager, but it defines the areas which should be covered in assessment. To their detriment, many programs are not based upon an empirical study of the manager's job as might be done through an analysis of critical incidents. They may be based upon a review of the research literature and judgments of executives about what makes a good manager; or worse, they may be barely modified copies of other programs. Without an accurate perception of the skills necessary for success in the position in question, accurate selection of personnel cannot occur.

The next step is to select the assessment exercises. They should be chosen with the following criteria in mind: (1) the decisions reached in steps one and two, (2) the exercises' validity, (3) the assessees' level of sophistication and education, (4) the relative importance of various dimensions, (5) the actual job content of the target position, (6) the need to observe important dimensions in several different exercises, and (7) the time available for assessment.

The fourth step in the procedure is organizational: the program itself and the assessor-training program are organized. In deciding which exercises to include, their order, the number of assessors needed for each exercise, the amount of time needed for each exercise, etc., the organizational staff should keep certain criteria in mind constantly: (1) the decisions reached in step one, (2) again, validity, (3) flexibility "to permit assessment of management potential at various levels and functional areas of specialization, and [to] provide for future alterations as the need arises," (4) comprehensiveness of the battery of assessment techniques, and (5) feasibility for the company's "structure and climate" and for the time allowed.[23] As for the design of the assessor-training program, the minimum amount of training would include discussion of the dimensions' definitions, practice in observing and recording behavior, interview practice, familiarization with the In-Basket, and orientation with the procedure for reaching final decisions. At the end of this organizational step, the program should then be announced, participants informed, and administrative matters handled.

After the fifth step, assessor training, has been completed, the program should be conducted and feedback given. Although not in a direct way a step in initiating a center, procedures for evaluating the program's impact and validating it against a criterion of job success should be set up and set in motion either concurrently with the program or at its completion. The importance of establishing rational validity or empirical validity cannot be overemphasized (see chapter VI).

VALIDITY

The internal evidence suggests and the external evidence shows that the assessment center method is valid. For internal

---

[23] Lee R. Ginsburg and Arnold Silverman, "The Leaders of Tomorrow: Their Identification and Development," *Personnel Journal*, Vol. 51 (September 1972), p. 663.

evidence, one can look to the nature of the rating process and to the nature of the exercises; for external evidence, one can look to the validation studies conducted so far. Although the internal evidence, the nature of the rating process and of the exercises, directly contributes only to the rational validity of the method, one must remember that the *cause* of the method's empirical validity lies in the rating process and the exercises. Without a sound rating process and sound exercises, the external evidence of validity must be negative.

The Rating Process

Despite the many unique features of assessment programs, the Overall Assessment Rating arises from a threefold process common to all. First, the dimensions or variables to be assessed are determined by studying the position for which the assessees will be candidates. Second, the candidate is given a *quantitative* rating on each variable: how much energy does the candidate display? how much leadership? how much organizational ability? etc. Third, the judgments are combined into an overall *qualitative* prediction.

The nature of the rating process certainly contributes to the high level of "face validity" of the assessment center method and accounts in part for its high level of scientific validity. The focus on the position in question, the sheer volume of information usually produced, and the mix of quantitative and qualitative aspects is impressive. More important, one review of all pre-1956 scientific validity studies of assessment center programs revealed that the OAR correlated with several criteria: the correlation was greatest for job potential, then for progress, and finally for performance.[24] Among the reasons for these correlations are the large amount of information generated in steps one and two of the rating process, the burden on the assessors to engage in considerable fact finding prior to decision making, and the conduciveness of the data to judgmental integration.

The Nature of the Exercises

The rating process, however, can contribute to the validity of an assessment center program only insofar as the exercises are designed to elicit behavior relevant to the position in question. Herein lies much of the strength of the assessment center

---

[24] Cohen, et al., *The Validity of Assessment Centers*, p. i.

method. At the assessment center, a candidate's observed performance is similar to the management role that he would have to assume, and the assessors need not make extended judgments; that is, the exercises are actually job samples. Whether to use signs or samples of behavior to predict subsequent job performance is a relatively settled issue in assessment. Samples of behavior, which form the core of assessment, eliminate certain problems caused by measuring signs of behavior. Faking and response sets are eliminated with behavioral samples because self-reports of attributes and interests are not relied upon. A charge of lack of relevance cannot be successfully levied against samples of behavior nor can a charge of "cultural bias."

A related issue is, Do people act naturally in assessment situations? On the one hand, people may do poorly because the situation is artificial. On the other hand, people may distort themselves to look good in the assessment situations. Fortunately for assessment, neither of these reactions is apparently a problem.[25]

> Situations are selected to be typical of those in which the individual's performance is to be predicted. . . . [Each] situation is made sufficiently complex that it is very difficult for the persons tested to know which of their reactions are being scored and for what variables. There seems to be much informal evidence that the persons tested behave spontaneously and naturally in these situations. . . .[26]

Validation Studies

The hope that the naturalness of the situations evokes valid responses has been confirmed by several validation studies. The most extensive empirical validation of an assessment center program in industry was done by Douglas W. Bray and Donald L. Grant on AT&T's Management Progress Study.[27] The focus was aptly chosen. Because none of the information collected about the subjects was ever given to company officials connected with the subjects, there was no criterion contamination; that is, the subjects' careers were not affected by their OARs. Table

[25] David F. Hoyle, coordinator—AT&T Management Assessment Program, interview at Woodhaven, Michigan, March 1975.

[26] John C. Flanagan, "Some Considerations in the Development of Situation Tests," *Personnel Psychology*, Vol. 7 (Winter 1954), pp. 462-63.

[27] Cohen et al., *The Validity of Assessment Centers*, p. 10.

VII-4 shows the relationship between the OARs and management levels that the college-educated and noncollege-educated subjects had attained by mid-1965. Of the former subjects, 49.6 percent had been judged to have management potential; of the latter, 28.4 percent. An additional study found that the predictive validities of this uncontaminated data were high; 82 percent of the college-educated who had reached middle management had been correctly judged; 75 percent of the noncollege-educated who had reached middle management had been likewise judged.[28]

The first validity study of Michigan Bell's PAP compared the men assessed with the first forty men promoted before the program began. Of the assessed group, 62.5 percent had received "better than satisfactory" ratings on the job; of the non-assessed group, only 35 percent had received that rating. Further, 67 percent of the assessed had been found capable of moving higher in management, while only 35 percent of the nonassessed had been found that capable.[29] (For a selected list of validation studies focusing on the assessment center method and for a sample of validity findings, see Appendix I.)

Differential validity does not appear to be a problem for the assessment center method. The research at Michigan Bell into the possible differential validity of its assessment program found *no* evidence of discrimination toward either minorities or women:

> The assessment dimensions can be grouped into identical factors for both white and black females. . . .
> Each assessment method produces evidence for specific dimensions—the source of evidence for the assessment dimensions being the same for the two racial groups.
> Interpersonal Skills (the group exercises) and Administrative Skills (the In-Basket) are most heavily weighed in the Overall Assessment Rating; Effective Intelligence (paper-and-pencil tests), the least.
> The assessors place similar weights on assessment dimensions when deriving Overall Assessment Ratings for whites and blacks.
> In terms of the relationship between the assessment dimensions and subsequent job performance, those dimensions predictive for one racial group are also predictive for the other.
>   . . .

-----

[28] Marvin D. Dunnette, "The Assessment of Managerial Talent," in *Advances in Psychological Assessment*, Vol. II, ed. Paul McReynolds (Palo Alto: Science and Behavior Books, Inc., 1971), pp. 79-108.

[29] Huck, "Determinants of Assessment Center Ratings," p. 8.

TABLE VII-4

*Relationship Between Assessment Staff Prediction
and Management Level Achieved by 1965*

Sample	Staff Prediction	No. at First-Level Management	No. at Second-Level Management	No. at Middle Management or Above
College	Will make middle management in ten years	62	1	31	30
	Will not make middle management in ten years	63	7	49	7
Noncollege	Will make middle management in ten years	41	3	25	13
	Will not make middle management in ten years	103	62	36	5

Source: Douglas W. Bray and Donald L. Grant, "The Assessment Center in the Measurement of Potential for Business Management," *Psychological Monographs*, Vol. 80, No. 625 (1966), p. 17.

A common regression line can be applied to the prediction of Overall Job Performance for both whites and blacks.

No relationship was found between assessment performance and an adjusted salary index, nor between the supervisory ratings and the salary index for either racial group.

Performance in the assessment program is directly related to performance in a supervisory capacity for both whites and blacks anywhere from one to six years after attending the assessment program. The predictive accuracy is even greater when assessment results are related to potential for advancement.[30]

The findings cannot necessarily be generalized to all assessment center programs, but because the Bell program has provided the foundation for many other assessment centers, the evidence is quite compelling.[31] As we mentioned in chapter VI, there are serious reservations about the existence of differential validity as a substantive phenomenon, but the federal government's new "Uniform Guidelines on Employee Selection Procedures," by incorporating the concept of differential validity within the definition

---

[30] *Ibid.*, pp. 116-17. (Emphasis added.)

[31] In July 1975, eighty-one subjects, of whom forty-six were minorities, were assessed in order to discover if the assessment process operated differentially for whites as compared to blacks. A rating of overall assessment performance and future potential was obtained. No evidence of discrimination was uncovered. Again, no definite conclusion can be reached because of the limited sample size, but the results support the findings of Huck at AT&T. George Russell, "Differences in Minority/Nonminority Assessment Center Ratings Studied," *Assessment and Development*, Vol. 3 (August 1975), pp. 3 and 7-8.

of test unfairness, makes the concept an issue with which to contend.

IMPACT: ADVANTAGES, DISADVANTAGES, AND COSTS

Besides the issue of validity, two other issues deserve careful consideration when the assessment center method is examined: the impact of the program on the participants and on the organization involved and the cost of the program. What effect does the program have on a candidate's attitude toward his work and his career? What effect does the program have on the assessor after he leaves the program? What effect is there on the existing management structure, on cooperative behavior in the company, and on the decision-making status of managers? Finally, what is the financial impact of a program on an organization, and what are the financial pros and cons of instituting an assessment center program?

Impact on the Candidates

Does the assessment center method decide a man's or woman's career on the basis of two days' observation, and are two days enough time for the decision? To both halves of the question, the answer is no. Again, management uses the assessment center program's recommendations to make a decision which is affected and may be completely determined by other factors— e.g., the candidate's past performance, exhibitions of initiative, etc. Although the assessment center method may have a decisive effect on management's thinking, the appropriate question is not, Is two days enough time for the assessment center staff to make its decision? rather, Does the assessment center method represent a more deliberate method than those in practice now? The answer is yes. The staff's recommendations are not made on the basis of informally gathered data or of unstated criteria, nor are they made after fifteen minutes' review of an employee's file or during a lunch hour. But to lessen the fear of affecting a person's career excessively with the assessment center staff's recommendation, the OAR should not express his "ultimate career potential," but only his qualifications for moving on to the next job.[32]

---

[32] Allen I. Kraut, "A Hard Look at Management Assessment Centers and Their Future," *Personnel Journal*, Vol. 51 (May 1972), p. 323.

Whatever the impact of the method on an individual's career, that individual is not merely a passive receiver of that impact. He reacts to the experience. Once nominated or once assessed as outstanding, candidates may regard themselves (so may their peers and management) as "crown princes," and this self-concept may affect their subsequent performance. Feeling that their management future is assured, they may lapse in their work; or management may treat them in such a fashion that their success becomes a self-fulfilling prophecy. But nomination by itself should not create a "crown prince" effect. Less than one-half of the candidates in most assessment center programs are rated as having management potential, hardly a large enough percentage to create crown princes. As for those who do well in assessment center programs, they "are more likely to move ahead, but these moves appear to be influenced by other factors." [33]

A more serious problem for individual careers is the impact of receiving a low assessment rating; some may feel that they have received the "kiss of death" as far as their future with the organization is concerned. This could result in some undesirable attrition, since the candidate may be quite good at his present job. Low ratings do not automatically deny promotions; but, a poor OAR will impede the first promotion. At the Michigan and other Bell System centers, assessees who received low OARs still thought the program was worthwhile, and there has been no large-scale increase in turnover rates. Other organizations have found that "separation rates of individuals at different levels . . . [indicate] that the proportions of low-rated people who left do not differ significantly from the proportions of high-rated people." [34]

Receiving a rating at all, low or high, is stressful for some people. If a participant believes that his entire career rests upon his performance at an assessment center, the stress may be overwhelming. There is no doubt that the process is stress provoking, and the anxiety generated may affect some people's performances; but the assessment center method replicates the job environment, and stress is not added where it is not relevant. Stress is often an integral part of a manager's job, and a can-

[33] Allen I. Kraut and Grant J. Scott, "Validity of an Operational Management Assessment Program," *Journal of Applied Psychology*, Vol. 56 (April 1972), p. 128.

[34] *Ibid.*

didate should be observed while under stress to see how he copes with it.

A recent assessment innovation, however, immediate feedback in a developmental session, shows promise in diminishing the harmful effects of stress and of receiving a low assessment rating.[35] With extensive feedback concerning his performance, an assessee's self-development through greater self-awareness is enhanced. There is even evidence that this developmental process occurs without adequate feedback. But assessment experts agree that, to maximize the developmental experience, assessees should take a larger role in the feedback process.

For reasons besides feedback, the assessment center method does have positive effects on the candidates whether they receive a high rating or low rating. By participating in an assessment center program, an assessee's attitude toward his company and his job may be improved. His perception of the center as a fair and realistic place to demonstrate his talents will color his perception of the company. At the J. C. Penney center for its product-service management, "a group discussion exercise was developed to simulate a staffing problem. The exercise led to the conclusion that the only feasible solution was for management to increase overtime, and the assessors believed that as a result candidates would have a better appreciation of management's reason for asking them to work overtime when they returned to their jobs." [36] Participation in an assessment center program aids also in employee training and development. Many exercises such as the In-Basket, group discussions, and management games were training exercises long before they were used in assessment centers. Through participation, a candidate will surely gain a better understanding of the position for which he is being considered and so be better prepared for the job.

Finally, what about the nonnominees? Should they feel that their opportunities for promotion are nonexistent because they are not getting a chance to show what they can do? The answer to that lies in the answer to the question with which this section on the impact on candidates began. Management uses the assessment center program's recommendations to make a decision which is affected and may be determined completely

---

[35] Kraut, "A Hard Look," p. 324.

[36] William C. Byham and Regina Pentecost, "The Assessment Center: Identifying Tomorrow's Managers," *Personnel*, Vol. 47 (September-October 1970), p. 23.

by other factors. Furthermore, because less than one-half of the candidates are assessed as having management potential and only a percentage of those are actually promoted, nonnominees should not feel that participation in the program is a sure ticket or a ticket at all into supervisory positions.

Impact on the Manager/Assessor

From his experience with the assessment center method, a manager/assessor can benefit greatly. An assessor's interviewing skills are improved, and his observational techniques are broadened. He gains an increased appreciation for leadership styles, group dynamics, and insights into behavior. His management skills are strengthened through working with the In-Basket problem and other simulations. His repertoire of responses to problems is widened. Normative standards by which to evaluate performance and a more precise vocabulary with which to describe such performance are developed.

Assessor training comes from the formal training program before the program starts and, more importantly, from actually applying the procedures. These new skills do have use on the job, e.g., in performance appraisal and interviewing. In fact, General Electric feels so strongly about assessment's training benefits that it has increased the number of assessors per assessee.[37]

Impact on the Organization

Despite its many apparent beneficial effects on the participants, the assessment center method is not without its critics. The method has been labelled a perpetuator of existing management structure, a breeder of conformity, and a failure in selecting diverse kinds of talent needed for the future.[38] It has been suggested that the method places excessive emphasis on competitive, rather than collaborative, behavior.[39] Critics have asked, "To what extent do assessment center staffs actually take the key managerial responsibilities for subordinates' assessment and

---

[37] Virginia R. Boehm and David F. Hoyle, "Assessment and Management Development," in *Applying the Assessment Center Method*, ed. Joseph L. Moses and William C. Byham (New York: Pergamon Press, 1977), p. 221.

[38] Kraut, "A Hard Look," p. 321.

[39] Daniel E. Lupton, "Assessing the Assessment Center—A Theory Y Approach," *Personnel*, Vol. 50 (November-December 1973), p. 16.

development out of the managers' hands, as the staff builds its assessment empire?" [40]

There is some truth in the accusation of breeding conformity; "men nominated to attend assessment centers [are] more likely to be lower in independence and higher on conformity." [41] An investigation into the matter of the method's breeding conformity found, however, that those who are "self-actualizers" and value independence are predicted more often by the method to be successful in management. [42] To overcome the problem of inbred conformity among the nominees to an assessment center program, an organization may employ self-nomination or peer nomination or both, rather than rely solely upon supervisors' nominations. One study has found that peer nomination is useful in identifying potential supervisory personnel and is also predictive of performance. [43]

Whether the assessment center method overstimulates competitive performance at the expense of cooperative performance is a red herring. The intricate relationship of the competitive and collaborative spirits in the human mind is an active part of almost all human enterprise, and the assessment techniques used in most assessment center programs reflect this fact. For example, the PAP's "Small Business Problem" and "Promotion Problem" together establish an equal premium on competition and cooperation. Furthermore, if the program is designed not merely to arrive at a recommendation on whom to promote but also to help participants through feedback to "formulate their own developmental objectives" or to redefine their career goals, the objection to any emphasis on competition is obviated. [44]

To any questions about the possible negative impact on management's decision-making prerogatives and responsibilities, we must reassert that the assessment center method is only a tool to be used by management in exercising its prerogatives and fulfilling its responsibilities. As mentioned before, the assessment

---

[40] *Ibid.*, p. 15.

[41] Kraut, "A Hard Look," p. 321.

[42] William E. Dodd, "Will Management Assessment Centers Insure Selection of the Same Old Types?" in *Proceedings of the 78th Annual Convention of the American Psychological Association*, Vol. 5 (1970), p. 570.

[43] Joseph Weitz, "Selecting Supervisors with Peer Ratings," *Personnel Psychology*, Vol. 11 (Spring 1958), p. 25.

[44] Lupton, "Assessing," p. 17.

center method cannot measure every dimension necessary to success in management. If a manager understands this and has been familiarized with the purpose and design of the assessment center method, he will recognize the recommendations from the assessment center staff for what they are—aids to the decision-making process.

The most forceful answer to criticisms of the assessment center method, however, is a list of the beneficial effects that a well-designed, validated assessment center program can have on an organization.

1. Identification of the criteria important to management success.
2. Provision of standardized data to be used in placement. (When a manager is faced with considerable differences between the requirements of a candidate's present job and those of the position for which he is being considered or with differences between the kinds of jobs which the candidates hold, the usefulness of standardized data cannot be underestimated.)
3. Early identification of managerial potential in the manpower pool. (Although criticized for overlooking some people, the method has not been criticized for recommending personnel who actually do not have managerial skills; that is, its validity appears strong.)
4. Improvement of the candidates through the method's inherent ability to train and develop and through the simulation of their self-awareness.
5. Facilitation of selecting minorities and women for supervisory positions.
6. Through accurate placement, a reduction of management turnover.
7. Improvement of the assessors' managerial skills.
8. Enlightenment of management to a flexible, multilevel aid to making decisions about human resources.
9. Formulation of the organization's development plan. ("At no other time in the assessee's experience with his organization will six upper management executives spend an extensive two to three hours discussing his strengths, weaknesses, and developmental needs." [45] At no other time will management be so easily provided with the opportunity to

---

[45] Dennis P. Slevin, "The Assessment Center: Breakthrough in Management Appraisal and Development," *Personnel Journal,* Vol. 51 (April 1972), p. 259.

assess deliberately and in a concentrated way the organization's pool of talent.)

Those are not all of the benefits of an assessment center program. Because of the method's ability to shape itself to so many organizations' different needs in making decisions about personnel, the real benefits are manifold. As we point out in the next section, the benefits may even be hidden.

What Does a Center Cost?

"When compared with most traditional methods, the assessment center is a much more comprehensive approach for the collection and analysis of data and, consequently, is more costly." [46] An assessment center program can be expensive even for profitable corporations. In addition to the housekeeping costs and set-up costs, the cost of lost man-hours is incurred. That cost varies, of course, with the number of candidates assessed, the management level of the candidates, the number and management level of company managers in training and on duty in the program, and the amount of time allotted for training assessors and for assessing candidates. Based on the assumption of six man-weeks of management time expended, a conservative estimate of costs is $500 to $600 per candidate for a typical assessment center program. [47]

We have assumed here that company managers, not professionals, are being used as assessors, for the cost climbs quickly if the company decides to depend on outside resources. Therefore, the cost of assessment may be lowered because managers with minimal training can effectively serve as assessors in place of highly paid professionals.

Other means of saving cost exist. Thus, an assessment center program is not beyond the reach of a smaller company. Organizations with limited resources desiring the benefits of assessment might employ such cost-saving methods as completing all possible procedures before arriving at the center, conducting exercises on company property over weekends, using abbreviated programs, and pooling resources with other companies in the same position.

But even without the cost-savings, the figures are not at all excessive when compared with the costs of outright managerial

---

[46] Wilson and Tatge, "Further Assessment Needed," p. 173.

[47] *Ibid.*

failure resulting in demotion or loss of the individual, or with the greater *hidden* costs of substandard management performance over the years. One must also consider that assessment and development are being combined, a further saving of time and money. The critical question is not whether assessment centers are too expensive, but whether their contribution to the validity of the selection decision exceeds that of paper-and-pencil tests, interviews, weighted experience measures, or other traditional devices. This question of the additional costs of assessment vs. its incremental benefits requires further study.

CONCLUSIONS

Despite its exponential growth in industry in the past, the assessment center method is just beginning to move out of its infancy. Necessarily, any summary of issues or any conclusions about the method are preliminary and interrogative. Some of the preliminary conclusions of this investigation are, first, that the assessment center method is a reliable, objective, and valid predictor of various criteria of management success, more valid than traditional, informal selection procedures. The method has demonstrated its highest validities when used for selection of first-line supervisors; the reason is that the supervisor's job requires abilities not found in craft jobs, and the best way to observe managerial talents among blue-collar workers is to place them in assessment's elaborate simulations. Second, procedures unique to the assessment center, primarily the situational exercises, contribute a substantial element to the prediction of management success and allow a wide range of managerial ability to be displayed. Third, the center is seemingly an objective nondiscriminatory way to upgrade personnel to first-line supervisory positions. The assessment center method has demonstrated its superiority in objectivity over the usual upgrading methods time and again; it has thus far proved nondiscriminatory, but this conclusion is still subject to investigation.

Also still subject to investigation are several questions which have been present throughout our examination of the assessment center method, whether in the foreground or in the background. Our answers to those questions have been as extensive as the state of research and the state of the industrial asssesment center program's development allow. The list of questions and comments that follows stands as a conclusion and an indication of subjects for future research.

1. Can Michigan Bell's Personnel Assessment Program be successfully applied in other organizations to select supervisors from the blue-collar ranks? If so, is that application a good idea necessarily? We have used the PAP as a touchstone here in describing the anatomy of the assessment center program, and there is strong evidence that Michigan's program can be used for other companies. Assessment center programs designed for supervisor selection and patterned after the Michigan center have exhibited high validities when used by other companies (see Appendix I). General Electric, Sears, IBM, Union Carbide, and Standard Oil of Ohio all found that first-line supervisors chosen by the assessment center method were better managers than were supervisors selected by other means. Although there is no doubt that the Michigan Bell model represents a significant advance in assessment and is quite promising, this should not preclude greater experimentation and innovation.

2. Are all assessment center programs free of racial and sexual bias? In our section "Validation Studies," we indicate that differential validity does not appear to be a problem for the assessment center programs studied so far. That is, those programs are as valid for blacks and other minorities as they are for whites and are as valid for women as they are for men. We cannot generalize about all assessment center programs. The possible presence of racial and sexual bias in any given assessment center program will always be a threat; human beings, with all their foibles, select the variables to be assessed and make the assessment. Watchdog research will always be necessary.

3. Although it is one of the more attractive features to organizations, is the use of line managers, rather than psychologists, as assessors a threat to the validity of a program? When an organization uses managers as assessors, it loses some of the psychologists' observational talents; but, when an organization uses psychologists as assessors, it loses the managers' familiarity with the position to be filled and the skills necessary for success in a particular company. Which is more necessary for valid assessment—the observational talent or the familiarity with the job and company? As mentioned before, the research available indicates the interrater reliability between professional and non-

professional assessors is high. That research, however, is limited; more is needed.

4. Is the extra information generated by the process worth the additional expense over traditional measures? No hard data are available to compare the incremental cost of selecting the "wrong" man with the extra cost of assessment. In making such a comparison, future research should consider also the training and development done in an assessment center program.

5. What are the long-term effects of an assessment center program on an organization? As more institutions begin to use the assessment center method for development, as well as for selection, trends toward more effective and efficient internal and external growth should be watched for: more efficient manpower planning, more effective development of positions and delegation of responsibilities within, and more efficient and effective expansion of the organization through the use of talent identified by the assessment center staff. Some of the effects of the assessment center method on an organization will be hidden or ambiguous because of other factors' influence on an organization's growth. But to organizations interested in validated selection methods that are cost-efficient and serve to meet government requirements, to select first-level supervisors, to develop employees' talents, to fill a newly created position, or to fulfill a combination of such purposes, the research into long-term effects would be worthwhile.

CHAPTER VIII

Selection by Testing

Because of management pressures to improve employee performance and tenure and to meet legal requirements, efforts have been underway at Honeywell, Inc., since the early 1970s to provide managers with effective and valid personnel selection devices.[1] It was recognized from the beginning of this effort that personnel testing is a superior tool to use if managers expect to select good performers, retain good performers, and avoid charges of unfair discrimination.

Underlying Honeywell's support for personnel testing is the belief that relevant information about jobs and job candidates can be gathered, analyzed, and correlated. The first step in this process is job analysis; the job is defined in terms of the expectations that management has of job incumbents' performance. These expectations are translated into "performance standards." Once identified, performance standards provide the "core" information about a job that is used to validate the tests which are used to gather information about job candidates to predict their relative suitability for the job and to predict their tenure.

This chapter describes the process that Honeywell uses to construct a validated paper-and-pencil test battery for a first-line supervisor's position in one of its factory operations. At the heart of this process is the development of performance standards for first-line supervisors.

TESTS AND PERFORMANCE CRITERIA

In recent years, there has been a general improvement in the quality and quantity of available tests that can be used for selection. For example, it is not difficult to obtain tests which give more information (more scores) and take less time to

---

[1] The validation study and process described in this chapter were developed for Honeywell by Lawrence G. Vanden Plas, manager, Employee Standards, Honeywell Corporate Employee Relations.

administer while almost the same reliability or stability of re-sults of earlier tests is retained. There is also a trend to tie together the results of a number of different types of selection instruments. As a result, most test validation problems are re-lated to finding valid and reliable criteria to which to relate the results of the selection instruments.

Objective Criteria for Performance

The most obvious criteria presented for use in many studies are objective performance numbers generated by daily opera-tions. Some examples of objective numbers are widgets per hour produced by a factory worker, time to repair a machine by a field technician, or sales volume for a sales representative. All these numbers, despite their "objectivity," have posed prob-lems. In the case of the factory worker, for example, there can be a conflict between the objective numbers and the subjective evaluation of performance because better workers are often given the harder jobs. In addition, better workers may even do such tasks as setting up machines for poorer workers of correcting malfunctions. As a result of good management and job assignments, therefore, production is maintained, but poorer workers may end up with the best production numbers.

A similar problem developed in Honeywell when efforts were made to measure and standardize the performance of field tech-nicians, a group of employees who are responsible for repair-ing sophisticated equipment. A committee identified each type of equipment and developed a logging system to track the mean time spent by a technician to repair each type of equipment. The data collected indicated that lower graded technicians spent considerably less time on almost every given type of equipment than higher graded technicians spent. A study of the results showed that the intervening variable was good management. In other words, simple problems were repaired by lower graded technicians, and complex and difficult problems were handled by higher graded technicians. Because complex problems usually result in more time spent on a piece of equipment, objective performance numbers suggest that technicians handling these more difficult assignments are performing at a level lower than that of less skilled technicians.

The problems that arise when using objective performance numbers are quite clear when the technique is applied to sales representatives' performance. Commonly, sales volume and percent of annual quota are used to measure a sales representative's performance. A discussion with any good sales manager will, however, produce considerable doubt about the validity of using such data in the selection process; sales figures (total volume or percent of quota) for a given sales representative are affected by a number of variables beyond his control, e.g., economic activity within the sales territory and the length of time that the company has been in the sales territory. Although a good sales representative should do better in a given situation than a poor one, the situation in which the sales representative is placed will account for much of the variance between management expectations and sales results.

There is an additional problem hidden in the use of objective performance numbers as criteria to which to relate the results of selection instruments. A performance number may represent a "composite" of many performance variables rather than depict a specific performance variable. Therefore, when composite numbers are used as criteria, they do not match well with specific predictors. This is especially true when considering the nature of people, performance, and tests.

The Nature of People. Most people either learn to eliminate their weaknesses or, more likely, to use their strengths to compensate for their weaknesses. This works well in a situation in which a trade-off is possible, but when a trade-off is not possible or only possible to a limited extent, severe problems can surface. Consider a situation in which both planning skills and technical competence are important for a particular first-level supervisory position. A person filling this position who is weak in planning may be able to keep work moving by applying better-than-average technical competence. Another person, in the same role, may compensate for weak technical competence by better planning. If either of these persons were placed in a situation in which a trade-off was not possible, questions would probably be raised about how either of these individuals became supervisors in view of their poor planning or poor technical skills.

Nature of Performance. Performance is discontinuous. Those who are considered good overall performers are generally employees who are successful at keeping their performance in some areas well above an acceptable level while trying to insure that their performance in other areas rarely becomes a problem.

This phenomenon has been described as the ability to "keep a number of balls in the air without dropping any of them."

Elements of performance are often more than discrete; they may also be in conflict. A typical supervisor's job requirements provide examples of such conflicts, especially in the all-important task of having work done by others. This means that a supervisor's successful performance is dependent on such skills as directing work and influencing, training, coaching, disciplining, and working with others. Other job requirements, however, may conflict with a supervisor's responsibility for these people-oriented activities. For example, a large share of his time may be consumed by planning and administration of hands-on work so that less time for "people" matters is left. Furthermore, there are times when a supervisor must communicate discouraging information to the very workers on whom he is counting to perform a difficult task.

Nature of Tests. Each test is designed to measure only one concept or variable whether the test produces one or more than one score. For example, a good planning test will minimize the effect of testing for reading skill and will not measure any knowledge of history or mechanics.

The development of a test begins with the construction and selection of test questions. Care is taken to insure that each question relates to the specific ability that the test is designed to measure. These questions are used to construct an initial test, which is then administered to a group under actual testing conditions. After scoring, individual questions are analyzed to determine their relationship to the overall test score. Questions which do not exhibit a positive relationship (internal consistency) are dropped, and the test and the scoring key are revised. This causes the final test to be even more specific in what it measures.

The significance of the above characteristics concerning the nature of people, performance, and tests is that they pose a number of problems for validation. A test that is meant to be specific may be relating to a nonspecific composite performance number, which, in turn, may be influenced by people's tendency to mask their weaknesses with their strengths. In addition, the discrete nature of performance tends to make composite performance ratings an attempt at mixing apples and oranges, especially when certain discrete performance factors are in conflict with each other. Thus, trying to establish a meaningful relationship between composite performance and a single testing instrument will probably produce little more than frustration. But performance ratings need not be composite numbers. They can be purified by identifying and defining each discrete component of performance. Once this is achieved, they can be related one at a time to various predictors (test instruments).

THE CONCEPT

Honeywell's testing program is based on the convictions that (1) discrete performance for a particular job can be defined and, with some degree of accuracy, measured; (2) information related to performance in a specific job can be obtained from a job applicant; and (3) information collected from a job applicant through interests tests, patterned interviews, etc., can be used to judge objectively the applicant's relative suitability for the job. This concept has a number of implications for upgrading and selection. First, the method can indicate what information about candidates is job related (valid). Second, it provides a structure for a more complete description of the job and a better matching of the candidates to a specific job. Third, because minorities and women may be at a disadvantage in that they have not had the opportunity for certain previous jobs or experiences (factors often used to evaluate candidates for first-level supervision), the method provides a means to evaluate the validity of past jobs and experiences, as well as to evaluate the validity of alternatives. Fourth, besides providing guidance to the candidates about what will be expected in the job, the performance standards provide essential input for training programs.

THE PROCESS

The process involved in developing the testing program and selection procedure for a Honeywell factory supervisor's position consists of three phases: performance standards development, predictor validation, and interest profile development. Some of the phases are coterminous with one another and even with the implementation of the testing and selection procedure. For example, Phases One and Two can, and generally do, occur simultaneously; and monitoring, auditing, and evaluation can occur during implementation.

Phase One: Development of Performance Standards

The first step is the development of performance standards. During this phase, personnel specialists capture the thoughts of managers concerning their expectations of an employee's performance in a specific position. Then, these thoughts are used to develop a set of performance standards that apply to the specific job. By limiting the standards to a specific position, rather than generalizing about a group of somewhat similar positions, the standards are more explicit and more extensive and provide a more accurate performance measurement. In short, the objective is to induce managers to express their performance expectations, to describe methods and results in their own language, and to reach a consensus on the relative importance of different elements of the job. This method also helps managers to reach a consensus on the relative desirability of different types of behavior on the job.

This phase is similar to Flanagan's Method of Critical Incident [2] in that it defines a job behaviorally. This approach is used for two reasons. First, it most closely communicates the thoughts that managers have about performance; second, it has shown good interrater reliability when properly conducted. A number of items, however, differentiate the Honeywell process from Flanagan's critical incident method: first, characteristics unique to Honeywell's performance standards method include the use of typical or common behavior rather than a single critical incident or occurrence of behavior; and second, an attempt is made to generate twenty or more comments or anecdotes about different types of job behavior that vary widely in their desirability. All comments that describe what an incumbent should do or what qualifications recruits should have upon hire are not included in this process. Only comments that report an observable form of job behavior are used. Other improvements have been also made to minimize such common problems as central tendency, bias, and "halo effect."

Identify Managers. The steps of Phase One are depicted in Figure VIII-1. The process of developing performance standards begins by identifying at least six managers who can provide initial data on job performance. These managers are selected according to their familiarity with the job under analysis.

---

[2] J. C. Flanagan, "The Critical Incident Technique," *Psychological Bulletin*, Vol. 51 (July 1954), pp. 327-58.

FIGURE VIII-1

Development of Performance Standards

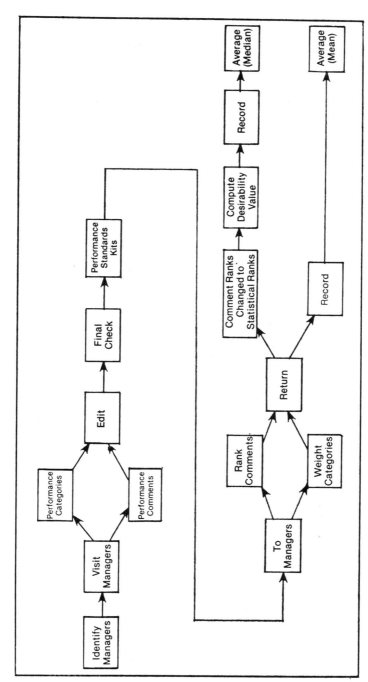

Source: Supplied by Honeywell, Inc., Corporate Human Resources Department, Minneapolis, 1976.

In nearly all instances, they are supervisors once removed from the job involved. Sometimes, managers two levels above the job are also included in the formulation of performance standards. Efforts are made, however, to minimize their involvement because they are less likely to be familiar with all aspects of the job and would not be able to contribute sufficient information about performance.

Group Discussions. In group discussion sessions consisting of at least two meetings, the managers selected provide information about their expectations of a factory supervisor's performance. If more than six managers are participating, an effort is made to limit the size of the sessions to four to six managers. The objective is to insure that adequate discussion takes place, and that each manager has an adequate opportunity to contribute.

The group discussion sessions are conducted by a person trained to gather information about performance. In those situations in which the job under study is geographically scattered and group sessions cannot be held, a trained person visits each manager and obtains the necessary information through a patterned interview.

Performance Categories. The initial objective of the managers' discussions is to collect information on "performance categories." Such things as job competence, control, and performance are subject to management expectations, and for each, a specific type of behavior which is considered important to overall job performance can be defined. Once identified and defined by the managers, these expectations and types of behavior are clustered into groups that relate to each other and, so, form categories. The performance categories developed for a factory supervisor are presented in Table VIII-1.

Performance Comments. The next step in Phase One is the generation of comments about each of the performance categories created. The "performance comments" are based on the key themes of the performance categories, as defined by the managers participating in the process. They are intended to be descriptions of behavior: good, bad, or neutral. Like performance categories, performance comments are the product of managers.

A method similar to the critical incident technique developed by Flanagan is used to collect performance comments from the managers. The objective of the procedure is to obtain a variety of comments about the way that job incumbents actually per-

TABLE VIII-1
Performance Categories for Factory Supervisors

1. Ability to plan for the accomplishment of goals (8%)
2. Ability to administer rules and policies fairly and consistently (8%)
3. Interdepartmental relations (6%)
4. Ability to train and develop subordinates (8%)
5. Initiative (9%)
6. Member of management (7%)
7. Technical competence (6%)
8. Human relations skills (10%)
9. Safety and housekeeping (5%)
10. Communications (8%)
11. Willingness to accept responsibility (8%)
12. Integrity, trustworthiness, and honesty (10%)
13. Department administration (7%)

Source: Supplied by Honeywell, Inc., Corporate Human Resources Department, Minneapolis, 1976.

Note: Appendix J lists coded evaluative statements for rating a supervisor's performance in each category.

form the job under study. Managers are asked to provide a broad description of performance in order that every conceivable type of behavior likely to be encountered can be identified, recorded, and valued.

During the collection of comments, the managers have a tendency to start with a few positive comments and then to proceed to and dwell on negative comments. When this occurs, the managers are guided back toward more positive statements. The greatest challenge, or difficulty, is collecting neutral statements. This problem simply reflects reality; desirable and undesirable performances are most noticeable and, therefore, are easiest to remember and to describe.

Most possible types of behavior are uncovered throughout the collection of performance comments. Sometimes, these comments describe behavior that is rarely encountered. In these situations, some managers often argue that the comment is not applicable to the job and should not be included, but it is important that most types of behavior connected with the job be identified and processed so that their significance and desirability can be objectively evaluated.

When a performance comment session has been completed, each performance category has a list of comments pertaining specifically to it. These comments cover an entire range of behavior, from least desirable (possible grounds for dismissal) to most desirable (performance results rarely achieved). The performance comments and performance categories are then edited.

Editing. The editing procedure is more than an effort to make the performance categories and comments more easily read and understood. It is also an analytical and judgmental step. The comments must be checked for clarity, especially in expression of desirability and undesirability. For example, if a comment describes a situation in a manner that makes it difficult to classify the behavior as desirable or undesirable, the comment is poor and must be rewritten or discarded.

Another objective of the editing process is to produce a list of comments that represents an adequate spread of statements of desirability. The goal is to have a fairly equal proportion of positive, neutral, and negative performance comments. The optimum number of performance comments for each category is about twenty. More than twenty comments is preferable to less than twenty. The actual number finally decided on, however, depends significantly on the type of performance being described.

Review and Comment. Once the editing process is completed, the edited performance categories and comments are distributed in the form of Performance Standards Kits to all the participating managers for final evaluation. Table VIII-2 provides an example of one performance category and the performance comments generated for it. This example is taken from the performance standards developed for the position of factory supervisor. The standards (performance categories and comments) are presented in their entirety in Appendix J.

Performance Standards Kits and Their Use. Once the performance standards for a specific job are defined in categories and comments, the relative importance of each performance category to total job performance and the relative ranking of performance comments according to their level of desirability must still be determined. These data are critical to the development of tools and the validation process and are the key to obtaining and effectively using performance ratings.

Performance Standards Kits are used as a means of obtaining the data necessary to establish values for performance categories and comments. These kits are simply a tool to aid managers in providing the required data. They consist of a group of envelopes, each representing a specific performance category and clearly labelled as such. Within each envelope are cards with a single performance comment typed on each one of them. Each card represents one of the performance comments generated for the particular performance category marked on the envelope. When these cards are drawn up, a random code number is assigned to each comment so that the comment can be tracked through the process.

Performance Standards Kits are distributed to all managers who directly supervise the job being analyzed (In many cases, managers two levels above the job also receive a kit.) This is unlike the initial step in developing performance standards, in which approximately six to ten managers were involved. The managers receiving the kits are first requested to take each envelope (performance category) separately and rank the performance comments contained therein according to their desirability. The comments are to be organized from lowest or least desirable performance to highest or most desirable performance. There is no forced distribution required in this exercise. Thus, a manager can assign one or more comments to the same level of desirability. In the unlikely event that a manager sees each comment as noticeably higher or lower than another, a perfect totem pole will emerge. More often, however, managers produce groupings of comments, which indicates that they believe that some comments are of an equal or near equal level of desirability. Compared to less experienced managers, more experienced managers tend to discriminate more (i.e., have more rows of comments) between levels of performance. Figure VIII-2 illustrates how two comment distributions may appear.

After managers have ranked the performance comments to reflect their desirability judgments, they are asked to number each card according to its ranking. The least desirable comment(s) is assigned the number one (1); each higher ranking card is assigned the number that reflects its ranking in comparison to the number 1 card. Figure VIII-2 illustrates this numbering process for situations in which a perfect totem pole is produced and in which a manager judges certain comments to be of equal desirability. Once all the cards have been numbered, they are returned to their appropriate performance category envelope. The manager then selects the next envelope, performs the process again, and repeats it until all the cards in each envelope have been ranked and numbered.

FIGURE VIII-2
Performance Comment Cards

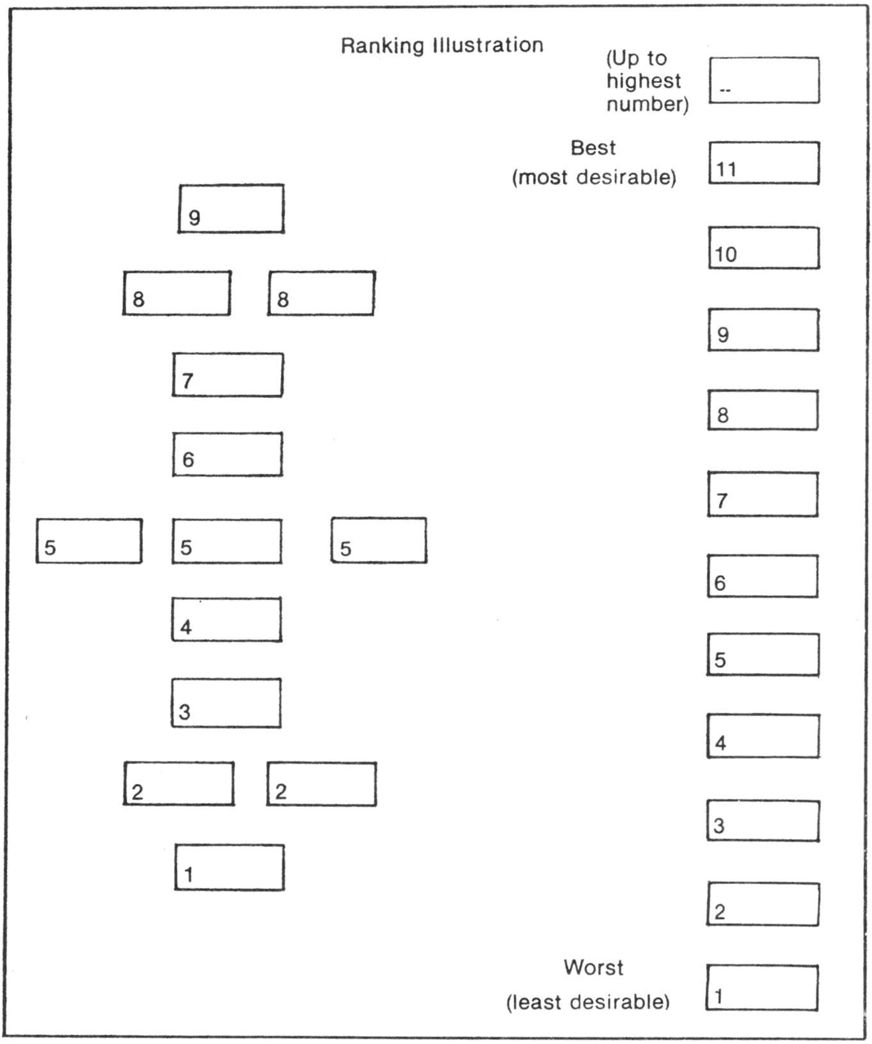

Source: Supplied by Honeywell, Inc., Corporate Human Resources Department, Minneapolis, 1976:

The second action that managers are requested to take as a part of their Performance Standards Kit effort is the weighting of performance categories. Although this is a simple process, it is quite significant and requires special handling. The weighting is done by distributing 100 points among the performance categories developed for a specific job. The points are distributed on the basis of the percent of total job performance. The kits include a weighting sheet which identifies each category and provides a space for recording distributed points.

The task of weighting the performance categories has special significance because certain variations in a particular job will exist throughout a given organization even though the performance categories are the same. For example, if there are first-line factory supervisors working in different departments within a facility, the relative importance of any one particular performance category to overall job performance is likely to vary. The weighting process takes into consideration these variations because managers are instructed to provide separate weightings for each variation of the job under study. The next step in the process begins when the performance category weightings and performance comment rankings are available for analysis.

The analysis of the performance comments consists of converting each card's ranking into an overall statistical rank, or "desirability value." Because the number of comments may vary among performance categories, and for ease of comparison and analysis, all comment rankings are converted to a 0 to 100 scale. This is done by dividing statistical ranks by the total number of cards ranked in the category. After the decimal points are removed, values fall on a 0 to 100 scale. A desirability value of 5 would indicate that the comment is very undesirable, while a value of 90 would indicate a high level of desirability.

Computing the performance category weightings entails calculating a mean value for each category. These mean values are rounded off to the nearest whole number so that the total point value for the entire job equals 100. An example of a completed performance standard (category and comments) with its computed weighting and desirability values is presented in Table VIII-2.

Phase Two: Predictor Validation

When what is to be predicted (performance standards, i.e., criteria) is clear, selection tools (predictors) can be chosen or

TABLE VIII-2

*Performance Category Weighting
and Performance Comment Desirability Values*

Category

Ability to plan for the accomplishment of goals. (8%[a])

Description of Category

Includes determination of subgoals to support company goals, anticipating possible problems, gathering relevant information, setting priorities, and implementing plans.

Comments

Adjusts to changing conditions and reacts accordingly; accomplishes his planned results. (96[b])

Is able to determine and set priorities despite interruptions from a variety of departments. (96)

Foresees possible problems and has contingency plans ready. (91)

Plans ahead, but remains flexible. (89)

Can differentiate a short-term situation from a long-term situation. (87)

Requisitions more or surpluses personnel when the work load changes. (77)

Good on short-range planning, but makes no long-range plans. (74)

Tends to overcommit himself. (54)

Makes plans before weighing all the facts. (54)

Plans do not take into account changes in the product mix. (54)

Is reluctant to delegate work which could be done by someone else. (46)

Is not adequately aware of company goals—both short- and long-range—when he makes his plans. (43)

Gets involved doing the work, rather than supervising it. (39)

Makes plans, but they are unrelated to company goals. (39)

Has difficulty meeting deadlines and hates to commit himself. (37)

Occasionally spends a day or more on small problems (e.g., tracking down a $1.80 change on his budget printout). (35)

Considers planning alone sufficient without action to implement it. (35)

Makes sure he always has enough work on hand, even if it means missing a schedule date. (31)

Plans come apart under pressure. (30)

Plans are usually grandiose and unjustifiable. (26)

Makes no plans, but reacts to the latest or loudest demands. (22)

Planning is incomplete and half-baked, many changes of direction. (20)

Every change is a crisis or disaster. (10)

Source: Supplied by Honeywell, Inc., Corporate Human Resources Department, Minneapolis, 1976.

Note: Desirability values are not given behind each comment, as shown above, for information purposes. In practice, each comment is followed by a randomly assigned code from a separate code sheet which relates to the desirability value.

[a]Category weighting.

[b]Desirability values.

developed, and validated. These predictors can be either chosen for study on the basis of their previously established success with a similar criterion or designed to relate to the criterion. This represents the starting point for the second phase of developing the testing program and selection procedure. This phase is presented in Figure VIII-3.

After a group of predictors has been chosen for study, it is administered for the purpose of validation to a group of employees who are incumbents of the job being studied. Utilizing the concurrent validation method (see chapter VI), performance ratings are also collected on these same employees. These performance ratings are typically conducted along with the administration of the predictors to avoid too much discussion of predictors before performance ratings are obtained. Using performance standards developed in the first phase of the process, managers one and two levels above the position provide the performance ratings on rating cards.

Performance Ratings. To avoid some of the problems inherent in collecting accurate performance ratings, certain procedures have been developed. First, the rating managers are informed in writing of what the performance rating is for and how the data collected will be used. They are also advised that the results of the validation study are completely dependent on the accuracy of their ratings, and that the ratings will not be used for any other purpose than for test validation.

Second, managers are provided with performance rating cards and are asked to fill out the information section of the cards for all the employees they rate. This section contains such information as name of person being rated, job title, name of rater, and number of months the rater has known the person being rated.

Third, managers are asked to finish rating all the employees on one performance category before rating anyone on subsequent categories. This last rule is intended to defeat at least partially the halo effect ("the tendency to let [one's] assessment of an individual on one trait influence [one's] evaluation of that person on other specific traits").[3]

Finally, managers are instructed to carry out the rating by using the performance standards (categories and comments) generated for the job. This is done by selecting a performance

---

[3] Milton L. Blum and James C. Naylor, *Industrial Psychology: Its Theoretical and Social Foundations* (New York: Harper & Row, 1968), p. 200.

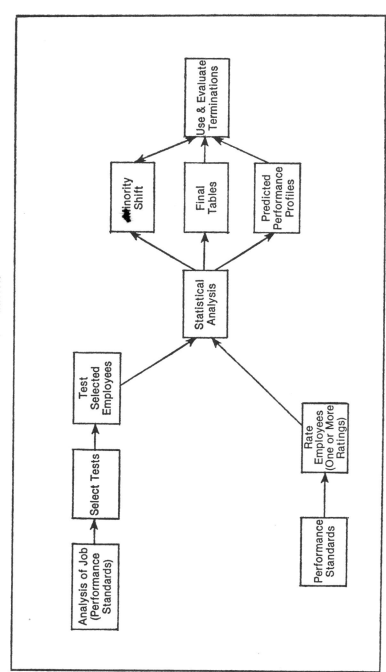

Figure VIII-3
Predictor Validation

Source: Supplied by Honeywell, Inc., Corporate Human Resources Department, Minneapolis, 1976.

category, reading its description, and then choosing that performance comment which best describes the employee being rated. Upon finding an appropriate comment, the manager is to place the comment's assigned code (random) number on the employee's performance rating card. As mentioned above, this process is repeated for each employee until all employees have been rated on a particular performance category; then, managers proceed to the next performance category and carry out the rating process again.

To simplify analysis, only one rating (performance comment) is selected per category for each employee. Managers are also told to use a question mark instead of a comment's code number if a category of performance cannot be evaluated. This minimizes collecting performance data of poor quality.

To decrease the halo effect further, the code numbers assigned to the performance comments do not give any indication of their desirability values. In addition, the proportional mix of positive, neutral, and negative comments are varied from category to category, and the group of undesirable comments is begun with very negative comments. This last measure eases managers into the rating process by permitting them to rate an employee as low (i.e., to assign him an undesirable comment) without having to rate the employee at the very bottom. In other words, a distribution of undesirable, desirable, and neutral performance comments assist managers and appears to reduce their tendency to rate all employees relatively high or low.

The large number of performance comments for each category also discourages managers from producing "central tendency" ratings. This is because there is no obvious or apparent central performance value. Additionally, multiple ratings are collected on each employee when possible. This is achieved by getting inputs from two or more levels of supervision and previous supervisors. Multiple ratings seem to encourage more accurate ratings.

Statistical Analysis. The most common statistical method used to evaluate the validity of a test or other selection device is correlation analysis. This means determining statistically the relationship between each predictor and each criterion (performance standard). When this method is used, the higher correlation coefficients are usually reported, along with a sociably acceptable test of significance. Usually all of the data will, however, have been analyzed without a scattergram's or scatterplot's being drawn. This is despite Downie's and Heath's warning "that a scatterplot should be set up every time one is computing a correlation coefficient, no matter what computing technique is being used." [4]

Early in the development of Honeywell's selection program, it was decided that, if so much effort had gone into the development of criteria and the selection or development of predictors, a complete effort also must go into analyzing the relationship between the predictors and criteria. As a result, a scatterplot is prepared to show the relationship between each predictor and each criterion used in the study. Because this often means that well over one hundred scatterplots must be prepared, a time-sharing computer terminal is used. The scatterplots graphically present the general trend of the predictor's and criterion's relationship. Although most commonly a positive, more or less linear relationship is found, a negative, or curvilinear, relationship is not uncommon.

Expectancy Tables. The more a predictor is related to job performance, the better it separates the people tested into different performance groups. The match of the abilities, interests, and other characteristics of an applicant to a particular job is, however, seldom absolute. Accordingly, selection information must be prepared and presented in a way that reflects its relative nature and must be usable and understandable for the average line manager.

A useful method of presenting probability data is an expectancy table or chart. Just as the weatherman gives the probability, based on available data, of rain's occurring, expectancy tables show the probability, given an applicant's scores on a test, of that applicant's developing into a particular type of performer. Predictor scores are meaningless by themselves and must be converted into probabilities to be plotted on an expectancy table.

Expectancy tables are specific to a predictor and performance category. That is, for each predictor related to a performance category, an expectancy table is developed. Because each performance category commonly has two or more predictors, each category will usually have two or more expectancy tables. An example of an expectancy table for a performance category and predictor is presented in Figure VIII-4.

---

[4] N. M. Downie and R. W. Heath, *Basic Statistical Methods*, 2d ed. (New York: Harper & Row, 1965), p. 79.

FIGURE VIII-4
Expectancy Table and Symbols

High Performers	20%*	51%	70%	75%
Low Performers	80%*	49%	30%	25%
Test Score Range	0-3	4-8	9-13	14-20

Symbols Used in the Expectancy Tables

Symbol	Explanation
o	None of the group of current employees who were tested had scores in this range.
*	The number of people in this range was so small that how it would divide between the performance levels could not be determined.
50%*	Based on the division of people between the performance levels and the total pattern of the data, a determination could be made, but an asterisk is used to indicate that it is based on a small sample.
51%	A percent without an asterisk indicates the percent of employees having a test score in the range listed below the percent who were described as being in that performance level. The sample was large enough to make a rather positive determination.
	The shaded area around any of the information on the expectancy tables indicates that the probability that the applicant has the necessary abilities to do the job is relatively low. Most applicants would do better. Doubts about their ability should be resolved by using other sources of information before further consideration.

Source: Supplied by Honeywell, Inc., Corporate Human Resources Department, Minneapolis, 1976.

Differential Validity. The federal government's 1978 employee selection guidelines state:

> Where a selection procedure results in an adverse impact on a race, sex, or ethnic group . . . and that group is a significant factor in the relevant labor market, the user generally should investigate the possible existence of unfairness for that group if it is technically feasible to do so.[5]

The term "technically feasible" is defined as the existence of conditions that permit undertaking meaningful criterion-related validity studies. These conditions include the opportunity to obtain unbiased job performance criteria and the presence of a sample of minority individuals of sufficient number to achieve findings of statistical and practical significance. As people involved in validation studies know, it is often hard to obtain a sufficient number of individuals, regardless of race, to achieve findings of statistical and practical significance. Although the lack of a sufficient minority sample eliminates the need for an additional validation study, it does not eliminate a company's desire to achieve its affirmative action goals even when faced with minorities' poor performance on the company's tests. Minority candidates often do not have the education, training, or experience of Caucasian candidates and tend to be at a disadvantage if paper-and-pencil predictors are used. The Honeywell testing program includes a technique to overcome this problem.

"Shift Factor." The "shift-factor" technique consists of matching the criterion scores of minorities (e.g., blacks) with those of Caucasians and then studying the match of predictor score means. For example, one study conducted showed that minority and Caucasian performance ratings matched on each performance category, but that there were significant differences in the test score means of the two groups. When this situation occurs, a shift factor, the average of the difference in test score means between the groups being studied, is used to narrow the differ-

---

[5] "Uniform Guidelines on Employee Selection Procedures," *Daily Labor Report,* August 25, 1978, Special Supplement, p. 12. "A selection rate for any race, sex, or ethnic group which is less than four-fifths (4/5) (or eighty percent) of the rate for the group with the highest rate will generally be regarded by Federal enforcement agencies as evidence of adverse impact" (p. 8). But see chapter X of our study for a discussion of the burden of investigating alternative selection methods.

ence. The factor is added to the appropriate predictor scores for all minorities (or other groups) who are evaluated by the predictor. By adjusting the minorities' scores in this manner, one can add those scores to the unadjusted scores of Caucasians to prepare expectancy tables.

The shift-factor procedure has been in use for over seven years and has worked well. When the rationale for the technique is explained, managers have no difficulty accepting and using the procedure. This acceptance has been aided by their interest in achieving affirmative action goals while improving the accuracy of selecting probable high performers.

Shift factors are not a complete substitute for a separate validation study for minorities. Nonetheless, they provide a far superior alternative to doing nothing because it is not technically feasible to conduct a separate validation study. For example, the technique has been used to provide an alternative when as few as six minorities were in the sample. In that particular situation, multiple ratings on the minorities helped increase the sample base to over fifteen predictor-criterion pairs. Furthermore, the use of multiple criteria and comparisons with an adequate Caucasian group provided enough data to indicate the amount of the shift and its repeatability for each performance measure.

There is, however, at least one major danger in the use of the shift-factor technique; namely, making the assumption that, if an adequate minority sample were available, the slope of the regression lines for both the minority and Caucasian samples would be the same; that is, that there is a consistent difference between the predictor scores of equal performers in the two groups. Figure VIII-5 illustrates this assumption. The letter "D" identifies the difference between the predictor scores of equal performers at different levels. If the slopes of the two lines were not equal, the underlying assumption would be wrong.

To handle this problem, additional data must be considered. The difference (the distance "D" in Figure VIII-5) in predictor means for both groups at low levels of performance (low criterion scores) can be compared to differences in predictor means for both groups at middle and upper levels of performance. Although these differences may not be the same, the variation may not be significant. In the end, the rules adopted for decision making and the way in which the data are considered are oriented toward improving the practical accuracy of the selection/

FIGURE VIII-5
"Shift Factor" Analysis

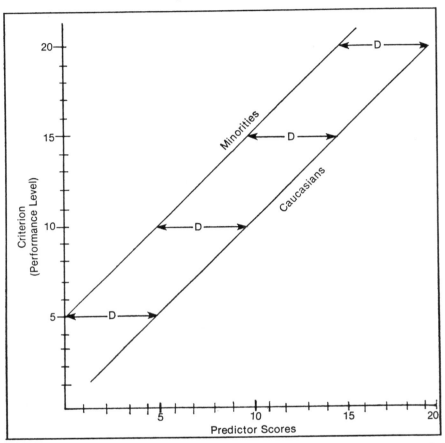

Source: Supplied by Honeywell, Inc., Corporate Human Resources Department, Minneapolis, 1976.

upgrading decision and toward the concern for fairness to candidates of all races.

Predicted Performance Pattern. The next step is to generate Predicted Performance Pattern sheets, which are single page forms that give key information for selecting the best candidate. Based on probabilities determined in the validation studies, Predicted Performance Patterns allow the manager to plot each candidate's probable strengths and weaknesses in relation to each of the performance categories. To simplify the data presentation, only the probabilities of a candidate's being a high performer are presented on these forms. In effect, the "high performer" portion of the expectancy tables is presented.

Figure VIII-6 is an actual example of one part of a Predicted Performance Pattern form. The part illustrated predicts probable performance in Performance Category I for a factory supervisor. The key words expressing the theme of this category are "Ability to plan for the accomplishment of goals." Immediately following the key words of the category is the category weighting, the indication of its relative importance. In this case, the factory superintendents have, as a group, concluded that performance in this category constitutes 8 percent of total job performance. The alpha codes along the left side of the bars indicate the tests that have been found to relate to the performance ratings in this particular category.

The bars are broken into segments, and each segment discloses the probability of a job applicant's being a high performer given the candidate's score on the predictor. Still referring to Figure VIII-6: (1) look at the bar across from MCT, the Bennett *Mechanical Comprehension Test*; (2) on the bar, locate a score of six; and (3) identify the probability value associated with the score. In this example, the probability value would be 50 percent. To the manager, a 50 percent probability value would mean that there is a 50/50 chance that the job candidate under consideration would be a high performer as a factory supervisor on that part of the job related to Performance Category I. From the standpoint of the validators, a score of six would indicate that, of those factory supervisors who scored in the six-to-eight range on the MCT, 50 percent were rated as high performers in Performance Category I.

With the exception of the first segment, the remainder of the MCT bar can be read in a similar manner. The zero in the first segment indicates that none of the concurrent validation sample had a test score in the zero-to-five range. This implies that either a person with such low ability scores had never been selected for the job or, if selected, the person was no longer in the position when the validation study was conducted. Thus, the practical probability of being a high performer with scores in this test range is essentially zero.

When a manager fills out the Predicted Performance Pattern form for a specific candidate, the appropriate parts of the bar

FIGURE VIII-6
Predicted Performance Pattern
Factory Supervisors Performance Category I

Ability to Plan for the Accomplishment of Goals (8%)

MCT	0	50%	67%	76%	88%
	0-5	6-8	9-13	14-24	25-60

EX	0	50%	67%	82%	90%
	0-2	3-6	7-10	11-15	16-30

EX-W	50%	68%	82%	87%
	17-30	13-16	9-12	0-8

PL	60%	75%	77%	100%
	0-2	3-6	7-9	10-20

Source: Supplied by Honeywell, Inc., Corporate Human Resources Department, Minneapolis, 1976.

Note: MCT is the *Mechanical Comprehension Test Form CC* by W. A. Owens and G. K. Bennett (New York: The Psychological Corp., 1949). EX is *Expression Form A* from the *Flanagan Industrial Tests* by John C. Flanagan (Chicago: Science Research Associates, Inc., 1960); the scores in this rank are the number correct; the scores in the next rank, opposite EX-W, are the number incorrect on *Expression Form A*. PL is *Planning Form A*, also from the *Flanagan Industrial Tests*.

(percents) are circled. Once completed, the form provides the manager with a picture of the applicant's performance pattern, specific performance category strengths and weaknesses, and overall probability of being able to perform successfully in the job. It is important to note that managers are not provided with cut-off scores or with only a few predictor inputs. The data are presented in terms of probabilities, and they are the result of a battery of valid selection tools.

The product of Phase Two, therefore, is a battery of valid selection tools that are used in conjunction with the shift factors and Predicted Performance Pattern forms. To maintain the battery of tests and to study further the validity of the predictors, regular reviews and evaluations focus on such items as retention, termination, transfer, salary history, and performance results.

Phase Three: Development of Interest Profile

In addition to probable job performance, most organizations are also concerned about the probable tenure of a job prospect. Honeywell, therefore, also conducts tests to measure occupational interest and to relate it to tenure. This development and validation of an Interest Profile for a particular job constitutes Phase Three. This phase and its result are quite similar to Phase Two and its result.

Figure VIII-7 indicates the steps of Phase Three, the first of which is to obtain and test a sample of employees with varied tenure and performance ratings. Because the primary goal is to develop a tenure prediction instrument for the job being studied, the employees composing the test sample are again the present job incumbents. The tests most often used for this purpose are the *Strong-Campbell Interest Inventory* or *Career Assessment Inventory*. Once the test has been administered, the tested group is divided into two groups on the basis of tenure and performance. Statistical comparisons are then made between the occupational interest patterns of long-tenure employees and short-tenure employees. Additional information is derived by comparing both groups of employees with "men in general" and "women in general." Data relative to these latter groups are provided by the publishers so that the general external comparisons can be easily made.

This statistical analysis identifies a number of occupational interest scales for which the test scores of the long-tenure group have different distributions than those of the comparison groups (i.e., the short-tenure group and the men- or women-in-general group). Much like the development of expectancy tables and performance patterns, the results of the interest analysis are converted into a series of bars. Profile sheets are developed from these bars, and managers use them to evaluate the match between a job candidate's occupational interest pattern and that of successful, long-tenure job incumbents.

Figure VIII-8 provides an example of some of the interest profile scales found on a Factory Supervisor Interest Profile form. On the bar (scale) labelled "purchasing agent," the small number under the center of the bar (i.e., 48) is the mean (average) score of long-tenure factory supervisors. The per cent above this mean is the per cent of long-tenure factory super-

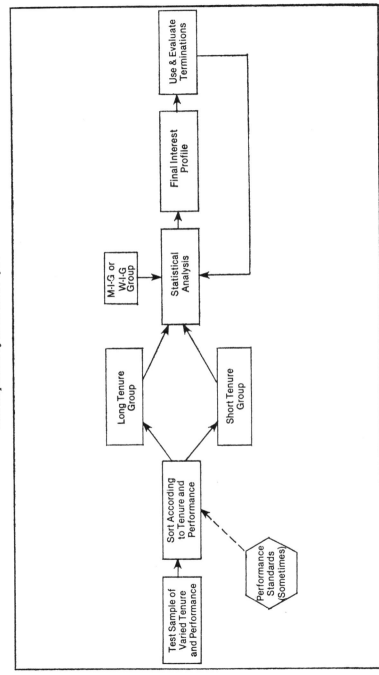

FIGURE VIII-7
Development of Interest Profile

Source: Supplied by Honeywell, Inc., Corporate Human Resources Department, Minneapolis, 1976.

FIGURE VIII-8
Interest Profile Scales
Factory Supervisors

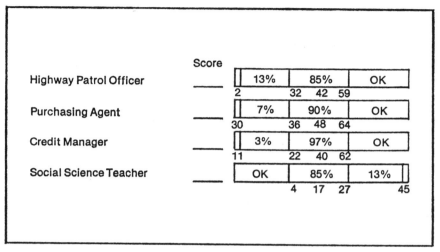

Source: Supplied by Honeywell, Inc., Corporate Human Resources Department, Minneapolis, 1976.

visors who scored between 36 and 64 on the "purchasing agent" scale. The double line at the end of the bar indicates that none of the long-tenure factory supervisors scored lower than that score listed below the double line. Thus, if a job applicant scored 32 on the "purchasing agent" scale, the candidate's score is below the scores of 90 percent of the long-tenure group, and the candidate should be considered questionable. If the candidate scores above 64 (the "OK" section), it merely means that the score is higher than that of most long-tenure factory supervisors, and that the candidate should be considered as suitable for the position as those who score near the average. The reader should not lose sight of the fact that this discussion involves only one interest scale, and that here the question of job suitability concerns only probable tenure.

As mentioned above, the comparison of job applicants' interest test scores is with the interest test scores of *successful,* long-tenure job incumbents. The word *successful* is emphasized because it is important to note that, in the interest profile, performance ratings are also taken into consideration. Because managers want to retain high performers, the comparison group upon which profile sheets are established consists not only of long-tenure employees but also of high-performing employees. Therefore, the predictor for the interest profile must identity the interests of probable high performers.

IMPLEMENTATION

In every case, the implementation phase begins with the presentation of the results of the validation study to the upper management of the division. This is followed quickly by the appointment of a selection committee chairman and the subsequent appointment of the committee. The committees generally consist of line managers and one personnel representative. Although the managers come from departments expected to need supervisors in the future and are selected for the committee for their competence, they are not all supportive of the approach to selection described here when they begin their work on the committee; however, they become rapid converts as they get involved in the process.

For the selection of factory supervisors, after the committee is formed and ready, a letter is sent from the general manager of the division to all hourly workers and office and technical employees whose salaries would allow a promotion to factory supervisor. The letter briefly explains the program and invites them to take the test battery off-hours. The most common test time is from nine to eleven on Saturday morning. (It has been said that the test time is the first test—determining who will show up on a Saturday morning on their own time.) The letter also explains that there are few guarantees in the program. Only those who come out on top when the results of all the tests are examined will be considered further.

After the tests, the top scorers' on-the-job performance and attendance, experience, and education are scrutinized, and these candidates are interviewed by two or three of the committee in patterned interviews. After all interviews are conducted, the entire committee meets and, taking into account all information, decides on the final pool. By this time, the tests may count for only about 20 percent of the final decision.

After the people in the pool are identified, they are offered off-hours, voluntary training opportunities, both individually and as a group, to further prepare them to be supervisors. The results of all training are added to a file containing all of the information regarding each person's suitability for a supervisory position. Those people who make the pool are assured that they will be among those first considered for all supervisory openings for which the pool is designed, i.e., all factory supervisor openings if the pool is designed to fill openings for factory supervisors. (Although superintendents or managers may pick anyone they wish from the pool, they must document in writing why no one in the pool is suitable before seeking someone outside the pool.) It is not uncommon for those in the pool to be offered different jobs which will help prepare them to be supervisors. But selection for the supervisory position depends ultimately on how well they prepare themselves and on the number of openings offered by business conditions.

CONCLUSIONS

In all instances in which this testing and selection program has been implemented, the results have surpassed initial expectations. One division which had a history of difficulty in locating and encouraging people to accept supervisory positions in the factory had over 150 people sign up to take tests. In almost every instance, the final pool offered enough females and minorities to meet the division's Equal Employment Opportunity goals. Another division which usually took three months to fill a factory supervisor's opening now fills them within a week. There have also been a number of side benefits. For example, the performance standards have provided the foundation for improved training programs and performance appraisal methods. These last two benefits have been welcomed by those who were supervisors when the programs were implemented, and many of the people exposed to one of the programs have spearheaded a move to apply the process to other positions.

Most important of all, however, is that the tests and resulting procedures have shown a strong ability to "pull people out of the woodwork." Members of the committees and management have been consistently surprised by the number of people identified by the process who would not have otherwise been considered. This has included people in administrative positions, such as accounts payable clerks, and, in one case, a person in a janitorial position. The objectivity of the process, plus this tendency to identify good people who would not otherwise have been considered, has caused the program to be highly regarded by the employees affected. This is even true for those not accepted into the pool. With subsequent counselling, they have realized that they would probably not want a supervisory position and have advanced to other jobs more suitable to their abilities and interests. Others are able to identify what areas need improvement and work on improving themselves for the next opportunity. The managers and employees feel now that the selection of supervisors is open and objective, and that anyone may try.

CHAPTER IX

The Assessment Center Method vs. Selection by Testing

It is evident from the two previous chapters that the selection-by-testing program and the assessment center method represent systematic and job-related selection methods that are guided by uniform and consistent procedures. Both methods are also research based and require some expert advice and assistance to construct, implement, administer, and maintain. These two systems thus differ sharply from those presented in Part One of this book. Yet, it appears that informal and unstructured supervisor selection processes based on tradition, impulse, or management assumptions are the norm in most American businesses, even though the selection-by-testing and assessment center methods demonstrate that selection and upgrading programs can be objectively and professionally based.

The assessment center and selection-by-testing methods, although equally impressive, represent two ways of addressing supervisor selection. Which, then, is the better method of upgrading and supervisor selection? Because a number of situational factors must be considered in answering such a question, including factors that are typically unique to a particular organization and beyond the scope of this book, no attempt can be made to answer this question. Some general statements, however, about the similarities and differences of the methods can be provided. This information can then be utilized by the reader to determine which method would be better suited for the organization in mind.

METHOD SIMILARITIES

Both the assessment center method and selection-by-testing program are founded on the same principle: objective, job-related

153

information can be gathered about a job and job applicant and related through the use of a measurement instrument. Furthermore, the information collected by the measurement (predictive) device can be used to predict the applicant's success in a particular job.

Accordingly, both methods are seeking objective, job-related, and predictive data that can be used by managers to make selection decisions. Each method encompasses research studies to validate the predictive ability of its selection instruments. More than one selection instrument is used under these methods, and this reflects the designers' belief that a battery of devices is preferable. Procedures are developed and used to guide the administration of each method and, thereby, to insure consistent application.

The need for professional, expert counsel and assistance to implement and maintain the selection system is common to both approaches. For the assessment center method, that need can be restricted to the start-up period, although a number of asssesment center staffs are led by psychologists or have them as members. It is apparent that acceptable results depend in part on the presence, constant or initial, of a person trained in statistics, psychometrics, and personnel staffing.

Another similarity between the two methods is the active, relevant role that line managers play in the development and administration of the selection instruments and procedures. Although not precisely in the same manner in each method, line managers help to identify criteria important to supervisory success. Moreover, they participate by using the selection instruments to aid them in making selection decisions.

The two selection methods are alike on another point: both are costly when compared with traditional, nonvalidated selection practices. The assessment center method, however, is the more expensive of the two. It is not difficult to understand why the methods are expensive. Their strengths make them costly, especially line-management participation, expert counsel, and validation research. The key question to be asked, however, deals with return on investment. Will the value of the results achieved through the use of either one or both methods exceed the costs associated with using the methods? Each organization will have to answer this question for itself. The value of making productive selection decisions and possibly of avoiding discrimination charges and suits must be determined by each organization considering the methods.

Finally, common to both methods is a periodic comprehensive audit and evaluation of the selection tools and procedures being used. A continuing validation effort is also common to both. These requirements are equally essential for any personnel selection program, but they are especially important requirements of selection programs that are to be research based, validated, and effective.

METHOD DIFFERENCES

The assessment center method is a "broad band" approach to selection; that is, it encompasses a number of selection devices to evaluate behavioral traits that are relevant to success in a particular type of job. In contrast, selection by tests is a "narrow band" approach that uses paper-and-pencil tests to measure psychological characteristics related to success or failure in a specific job. Because assessment centers include paper-and-pencil tests, as well as situational exercises, interviews, peer and self ratings, and business games, some professionals consider them to be superior to selection by testing.

The basis for the validation of both the Bell System's assessment center and the Honeywell selection technique is job (criterion) behavior. Under the assessment center method, the job behavior of first-level supervisors is described with specific variables that are considered important to management success, and candidates for first-level supervisor are assessed against these standard variables.

In contrast, Honeywell's testing and selection program defines performance standards for a specific first-level supervisory position in a specific organization. It then develops validated paper-and-pencil tests for the position to measure whether a candidate possesses the abilities and interests to perform successfully in that particular job. In other words, Honeywell's performance standards are peculiar to a first-level supervisory position, while the management variables utilized in the assessment center may cover more than one first-level supervisory position.

Tables IX-1 and IX-2 present the similarities and differences between the assessment variables used by Michigan Bell's assessment center and the performance standards used in Honeywell's selection-by-testing program. The differences identified in Table IX-2 stem from the two factors that make performance standards and assessment variables different. First, although assess-

TABLE IX-1
Management Dimensions and Performance Standards Similarities

Bell System's "Management Dimensions"	Honeywell's "Performance Standards" (Factory Foreman)
Managerial identification	Policy administration and discipline Member of management
Forcefulness	Ability to motivate, train, and develop subordinates Human relations skills
Likeability	Human relations skills
Leadership	Initiative and willingness to accept responsibility Ability to motivate, train, and develop subordinates
Organizing and planning	Planning and scheduling
Decision making	Department administration
Oral communications skill	Communications
Written communications skill	Communications

TABLE IX-2
Management Dimensions and Performance Standards Differences

Bell System's "Management Dimensions"	Honeywell's "Performance Standards" (Factory Foreman)
Behavior flexibility Energy Resistance to stress Inner work standards Self-objectivity Range of interest Scholastic aptitude Awareness of social environment Need for superior approval Need for peer approval	No Match
No Match	Interdepartmental relations Job knowledge, judgment, and technical empathy Safety and housekeeping Integrity, trustworthiness, and honesty

ment variables are characteristics considered important to being a good supervisor, performance standards are items which managers one to two levels removed from a supervisory job have determined as essential to success in a specific supervisory job. The second factor that explains the differences is that assessment variables encompass traits, abilities, qualities, and performance considered characteristic of being a good manager. Performance standards, in contrast, are specific measurements of job execution or achievement in a particular job.

CONCLUSIONS

We have already noted that both methods are expensive when compared to typical selection practices. Assessment centers are, however, considerably more costly to administer than the selection-by-testing program is. In contrast to the estimated $500 to $600 per candidate associated with an assessment center, a selection-by-testing program can be administered for about $10 per candidate. The housekeeping, set-up, professional staff, and management time costs associated with assessment centers account for this large difference. But whether one method is superior to the other for the purposes envisioned must be left to managerial determination.

PART THREE

Concluding Comments

CHAPTER X

Disadvantaged Upgrading and Legal Considerations

Despite our finding that formal supervisor selection systems for upgrading first-line supervisors are not typical in industry, there definitely are industry programs designed to insure that supervisor selection occurs on a systematic and valid basis. Two programs that have this capability are the assessment center program and the selection-by-testing program. There is substantial evidence that both have been successfully instituted in more than just a few organizations.

There is a new and growing interest in techniques used to select supervisors, an interest that stems mainly from the public objective to bring about the upward mobility of minorities, females, and other disadvantaged groups, especially into management positions. The usefulness of selection techniques in helping to achieve this objective is determined in part by the extent to which they promote or impede upgrading.

As has been documented by numerous court cases and research reports,[1] there is sufficient cause for the government's concern about unfair discrimination practices in supervisor selection. This has resulted in a close examination of supervisor selection methods by the courts and by federal and state equal employment opportunity agencies. These implications and legal considerations are discussed in the remaining pages of this book.

DISADVANTAGED POTENTIAL

If one views staffing as "an integrated system for moving people into, through, and, eventually, out of an organization,"[2]

---

[1] See Racial Policies of American Industry Series published by The Industrial Research Unit, The Wharton School, University of Pennsylvania, which discloses that American industry traditionally has given little attention to the matter of racially discriminatory supervisor selection processes.

[2] Lewis E. Albright, "Staffing Policies and Strategies," in *American Society for Personnel Administration Handbook of Personnel and Industrial Rela-*

the implications of selection for upgrading become self-evident. Both selection and upgrading are components of staffing, and upgrading efforts ultimately depend on the selection process for their success. This vital linkage is what makes a thorough study and understanding of selection and staffing so important for those responsible for upgrading programs.

The data and information presented in this study are also of significant value to programs whose mission is to upgrade the disadvantaged to meaningful jobs, especially if the target position is first-line supervisor. In addition to demonstrating two validated selection methods, we have provided information about the dimensions and performance standards for first-line supervisory positions. These must be taken into account when developing training programs for the disadvantaged if a realistic analysis is to be made of the capabilities and availabilities of the disadvantaged for promotion.

The assessment center method and selection-by-testing program can also provide a means for identifying the supervisory potential of disadvantaged persons. With the ability to obtain this type of information, manpower administrators can construct tailor-made human resource plans, as well as counselling and development programs. Clearly, this capability will improve the effectiveness of upgrading programs and, thereby, increase the chance that disadvantaged persons will be successfully promoted into and retained in meaningful jobs.

LEGAL CONSIDERATIONS

In enacting Title VII of the Civil Rights Act of 1964, Congress acted to avoid any implication that testing per se was either discriminatory or illegal under Title VII. The following amendment, offered by Senator John Tower of Texas, was enacted as part of Section 703 (h) in order to clarify the status of job testing:

> . . . nor shall it be an unlawful employment practice for an employer to give and to act upon the results of any professionally developed ability test provided that such test, its administration or action upon the results is not designed, intended or used to discriminate because of race, color, religion, sex or national origin.[3]

---

tions, Vol. I, *Staffing Policies and Practices*, ed. Dale Yoder and Herbert G. Heneman, Jr. (Washington, D.C.: Bureau of National Affairs, Inc., 1974), p. 4-2.

[3] U.S., Senate, *Congressional Record*, June 13, 1964, p. 13724.

The task of interpreting Title VII initially fell to the Equal Employment Opportunity Commission (EEOC), which issued its first guidelines in 1966.[4] The Department of Labor's Office of Federal Contract Compliance Programs (OFCCP) issued a similar set of guidelines in 1968.[5] In 1978 four federal agencies joined in issuing a set of uniform guidelines. Two main themes emerge from these guidelines. First, a test must bear a demonstrable relationship to successful performance of the job for which the applicants are being considered. Second, evidence of a test's validity should consist of empirical data demonstrating that the test is predictive of or significantly correlated with important elements of work behavior which comprise or are relevant to the job or jobs for which candidates are being evaluated.

Because testing instruments have traditionally acted as a bar to minority job candidates, "tests" were the first selection tools to come under close scrutiny by the federal agencies. Although these agencies focused their attention on educational requirements and on timed paper-and-pencil tests which produced a score, the OFCCP guidelines defined "test" very broadly so as to include all other

> . . . formal, scored, quantified or standardized techniques of assessing job suitability including, for example, personal history and background requirements which are specifically used as a basis for qualifying or disqualifying applicants or employees, specific educational or work history requirements, scored interviews, biographical information blanks, interviewers' rating scales and scored application forms.[6]

Two major legal issues have arisen over testing and the requirements of Title VII. First, there is the question of whether intent or effect is central to discrimination. Second, there is the question of what degree of deference should be accorded the federal agencies' guidelines. With a plethora of federal cases in this area, these two issues still remain largely unresolved.

Griggs v. *Duke Power Company*,[7] the first case to challenge an employer's use of educational requirements, came before the

---

[4] U.S., Equal Employment Opportunity Commission, "Guidelines on Employee Selection Procedures," 29 *Code of Federal Regulations (C.F.R.)* § 1607.

[5] U.S., Department of Labor, Office of Federal Contract Compliance Programs, "Employee Testing and Other Selection Procedures," as amended, *Federal Register* 36, Part 60-3, October 2, 1971, pp. 19307-10.

[6] *Ibid.*, Part 60-3.2, p. 19307.

[7] *Griggs* v. *Duke Power Company*, 401 U.S. 424 (1971).

United States Supreme Court in 1971. In *Griggs,* the employer had a policy of requiring that all *new* hires have a high school degree or its equivalent or attain a score on two tests equal to or better than the average high school graduate. The Duke Power Company of North Carolina, which had admittedly discriminated against blacks prior to 1965, had not conducted any exercise resembling a validation study of its selection measures.

The plaintiffs in *Griggs* argued that the company's policy was discriminatory because blacks were less likely than whites to have graduated from high school. The testing was alleged to be discriminatory because the "passing scores" were based on a national sample, which tend to be higher than those based on a southern sample. At the trial level, the court found that white employees hired without a high school degree or "passing" test scores were performing the job and were as promotable as those with a high school degree or its equivalent.

The company argued that the requirement was based on business necessity, the need to continue its promotion-from-within policy. The company contended that the requirements were applied fairly and consistently to both racial groups, and that it did not use the requirements intentionally to discriminate against blacks.

The Supreme Court in *Griggs* held that Title VII of the Civil Rights Act of 1964 prohibits the use of tests that operate to exclude members of minority groups, unless the employer demonstrates that the procedures are substantially related to job performance. The Court's ruling in *Griggs* was interpreted as holding that discriminatory intent need not be shown to establish a Title VII violation. In addition, the *Griggs* decision was viewed as indicating to the federal courts that considerable deference should be accorded the EEOC's interpretation of the meaning of Title VII.

As the first case involving Section 703 (h), *Griggs* was greeted with great interest. It was bound to be given broad application by lower courts, and this tendency was heightened by the expansive wording of the Supreme Court's opinion. Some people erroneously read the Court's ruling to mean that tests per se were illegal. In the aftermath of *Griggs,* testing measures which resulted in disproportionately low numbers of minority and female hires were presumed invalid. A careful reading of *Griggs,* however, does not produce this impression, for the Court specifically stated:

Congress has not commanded that the less qualified be preferred over the better qualified simply because of minority origins. Far from disparaging job qualifications as such, Congress has made such qualifications the controlling factor, so that race, religion, nationality and sex become irrelevant.[8]

The impact of *Griggs* v. *Duke Power Company* was dramatic. Companies were prompted to scrutinize their employment qualification requirements for job relatedness. As a result, many employment selection measures were dropped. In addition to eliminating artificial barriers to minority employment, test validation resulted in companies' making better selection decisions.

Two other Supreme Court cases bear on selection by testing and the EEOC's guidelines. In *Albemarle Paper Company* v. *Moody*,[9] the Supreme Court strongly reaffirmed its earlier decision in *Griggs* in a case involving seniority, testing, and back pay issues. In discussing the burden of proof in a testing case,[10] the Court stated that the plaintiff must first make out a prima facie case of discrimination, i.e., he must show that the test in question selects candidates for hire or promotion in a racial, ethnic, sexual, or religious pattern significantly different from that of the pool of candidates. Once a prima facie case is made out, the employer must show that the test in question is job related. Then, the plaintiff can "show that other tests or selection devices, without a similarly undesirable . . . effect, would also serve the employer's legitimate interest in 'efficient and trustworthy workmanship.' "[11] The Court's decision in *Albemarle Paper* is particularly interesting because it implicitly reversed the burden expressed in the EEOC's guidelines. The 1978 uniform guidelines likewise place this burden on the employer.

The most recent Supreme Court case involving qualifying tests is *Washington* v. *Davis*,[12] which challenged the validity of a qualifying test administered by the District of Columbia Metropolitan Police Department to police applicants. Developed by the Civil Service and designed to test verbal ability, "Test 21" had been used throughout the Civil Service. The plaintiffs did not claim intentional discrimination. They argued only that "Test

---

[8] *Id.* at 436.

[9] *Albemarle Paper Company* v. *Moody*, 422 U.S. 405 (1975).

[10] *Id.* at 425.

[11] *Id.* at 425.

[12] *Washington* v. *Davis*, 426 U.S. 229 (1976).

21" bore no relationship to job performance, and that it had a highly discriminatory impact on blacks. "Test 21" had been validated against performance in the police-training course.

When *Washington* v. *Davis* was before the district court, the federal district judge had concluded that

> . . . Test 21 was directly related to the requirements of the police training program and that a positive relationship between the test and training-course performance was sufficient to validate the former, wholly aside from its possible relationship to actual performance as a police officer.[13]

The court of appeals disagreed. The circuit court looked to the EEOC's guidelines which stated that tests must be validated against job performance. Since "Test 21" was not validated against job performance, the court of appeals held that it could not be used.

The Supreme Court, however, ruled that the court of appeals had used the wrong standards. Since the D.C. Metropolitan Police Department was a public employer not covered by Title VII prior to 1972, the plaintiffs had based their claim on the Due Process Clause of the Fifth Amendment. The Supreme Court held that the constitutional standard for adjudicating claims of racial discrimination is not identical with standards applicable under Title VII. The Court added that validation under Title VII

> . . . involves a more probing judicial review of, and less deference to, the seemingly reasonable acts of administrators and executives than is appropriate under the Constitution where special racial impact, without discriminatory purpose, is claimed.[14]

Even though the Supreme Court made it clear that Title VII standards for valid testing place a greater burden on the private employer, *Washington* v. *Davis* is viewed by some as having important implications because of the Court's attitudes revealed therein. In commenting on the district court's conclusion that the positive relationship between the test and training-course performance was sufficient to validate the test, the Court noted: "it seems to us the much more sensible construction of the job-relatedness requirement."[15]

---

[13] *Id.* at 250.

[14] *Id.* at 247. The Court is referring here to federal, state, and local administrators acting in an official capacity.

[15] *Id.* at 251.

As more decisions like *Albemarle Paper* and *Davis* are handed
down, the legal requirements for tests and validation will be more
clearly defined. There is little doubt that these decisions will
support those requirements which make it necessary for employers to continue justifying employment decisions on the basis
of empirical data when such decisions are believed to have an
adverse impact on a minority group. Question remains, however, about the extent to which the courts will be willing to
recognize as valid certain employment qualifications which do
not meet every technical aspect of the uniform guidelines.

Until 1978, two conflicting sets of guidelines regulated the use
of employee selection procedures. The EEOC had adhered to its
1970 set of guidelines, which was republished in 1976.[16] Those
guidelines were applicable to all employers covered by Title VII
of the Civil Rights Act of 1964, as amended. In 1976, the
OFCCP, the Department of Justice, and the Civil Service Commission adopted the "Federal Executive Agency Guidelines." [17]
The FEA guidelines covered all private and public government
contractors subject to Executive Order 11246, and all federal,
state, and local agencies whose EEO compliance is controlled by
the Civil Service Commission.

Many employers found themselves subject to both sets of guidelines, yet the EEOC guidelines and the FEA guidelines differed
significantly in several fundamental aspects. In 1976, the EEOC
refused to join the other federal bodies in adopting the FEA
guidelines even though professional associations [18] stated that the
FEA guidelines more nearly conformed to professional testing
standards than did the "unworkable" EEOC guidelines. In 1977,
the EEOC joined the OFCCP, the Department of Justice, and the
U.S. Civil Service Commission in proposing the "Uniform Guidelines on Employee Selection Procedures." [19] These guidelines, published August 25, 1978, represent a compromise between the EEOC
and the FEA guidelines. The new guidelines have been intensely
debated; several sections have met with severe employer opposition,

---

[16] "Guidelines on Employee Selection Procedures," *Federal Register* 41,
November 24, 1976, pp. 51984-86.

[17] "Federal Executive Agency Guidelines on Employee Selection Procedures," *Federal Register* 41, November 23, 1976, pp. 51734-59.

[18] *Ibid.*, p. 51734.

[19] "Uniform Guidelines on Employee Selection Procedures," *Daily Labor
Report*, August 25, 1978, Special Supplement, p. 1.

and they will undoubtedly be litigated. In several areas, the uniform guidelines clash with court decisions and professional standards.

Section 3B of the 1978 guidelines states:

> Where two or more selection procedures are available which serve the user's legitimate interest in efficient and trustworthy workmanship, and which are *substantially equally valid* for a given purpose, the user should use the procedure which has been demonstrated to have the lesser adverse impact. Accordingly, whenever a validity study is called for by these guidelines, the *user should include, as a part of the validity study, an investigation* of suitable alternative selection procedures and suitable alternative methods of using the selection procedure which have as little adverse impact as possible, to determine the appropriateness of using or validating them in accord with these guidelines.[20]

As noted above, the Supreme Court in *Albemarle Paper* v. *Moody* stated that the burden of choosing suitable alternative selection measures was on the job candidate once the employer had shown that the test was validated against job performance. Section 3B, however, reverses the burden as formulated in *Albemarle Paper*. In addition, the somewhat ambiguous wording of the guideline seems to relax the standard which a suitable alternative must meet. In *Albemarle Paper*, the Supreme Court appeared to indicate that an alternative must be at least equally valid before its nonuse will be considered discriminatory. The guideline suggests that an alternative with something less than equal validity should be used.

Section 14B(8), fairness of the selection procedure, incorporates the theory of differential validity, which we discussed in chapter VI. The theory that tests valid for one group, such as whites, might be less valid for a disadvantaged group, such as blacks, was quickly popularized in the late 1960s. According to the theory, some culturally deprived groups might score lower on tests but perform as well on the job as those who scored higher on the test. This untested theory was incorporated into the EEOC's 1970 guidelines, which were issued without provision for comment. In studies conducted subsequent to the issuance of the 1970 guidelines, there has been no substantial evidence to support the theory of differential validity.[21]

---

[20] *Ibid.*, p. 8 (Emphasis added.)

[21] See Joel T. Campbell et al., *An Investigation of Sources of Bias in the Prediction of Job Performance: A Six-Year Study* (Princeton, N.J.: Educational Testing Service, 1973); Lloyd G. Humphreys, "Statistical Definitions

Even now that the uniform guidelines are adopted, it is difficult to predict how employers will respond to guidelines which do not conform with professional standards. In *Griggs* v. *Duke Power Company,* the Supreme Court stated that the EEOC guidelines are "no doubt entitled to great deference." [22] Yet, in *Espinoza* v. *Farah Manufacturing Company,*[23] the Supreme Court rejected an EEOC guideline which declared discrimination against aliens unlawful as a form of discrimination based on national origin. In *Espinoza,* a Texas employer, who refused to hire aliens, employed a disproportionately high number of Mexican-Americans. In refusing to enforce the EEOC guideline, the Court stated, "courts need not defer to an administrative construction of a statute where there are 'compelling indications that it is wrong.' " [24]

FINAL COMMENT

The first-line supervisor represents the highest rank to which many blue-collar workers can aspire. Judging by our study, most selection procedures are largely informal and often entirely subjective. An ancillary result of the push for equal employment opportunity seems to be an increased tendency of companies to formalize and to increase the objectivity of their upgrading systems, and this appears to be salutary.

---

of Test Validity for Minority Groups," *Journal of Applied Psychology,* Vol. 58 (August 1973), pp. 1-4; Frank L. Schmidt et al., "Racial Differences in Validity of Employment Tests: Reality or Illusion?" *Journal of Applied Psychology,* Vol. 58 (August 1973), pp. 5-9; Edward J. O'Connor et al., "Single-Group Validity: Fact or Fallacy?" *Journal of Applied Psychology,* Vol. 60 (June 1975), pp. 352-55.

[22] 401 U.S. 431 (1971).

[23] *Espinoza* v. *Farah Manufacturing Co., Inc.,* 414 U.S. 86 (1973).

[24] *Id.* at 94-95.

APPENDIX A

Industrial Relations Department
Interview Form

I. General: History of the Plant

1. Has this plant recently experienced any major hirings or layoffs? _____Yes _____No

   If yes, please specify.

2. In the last three years, has this plant encountered any personnel problems with respect to:

   a. absenteeism?   _____Yes   _____No
   b. race relations?   _____Yes   _____No
   c. disciplinary problems?   _____Yes   _____No
   d. youth?   _____Yes   _____No
   e. tardiness?   _____Yes   _____No
   f. turnover?   _____Yes   _____No
   g. morale?   _____Yes   _____No

   If yes, please explain.

3. In the last three years, have you encountered any strikes? _____Yes _____No

4. How would you describe union-management relations at this plant?

5. Description of local labor market conditions: unemployment, racial composition, ability to attract workers from outside the immediate area, skill level, etc.

6. What mechanism does this plant use to measure affirmative action results?

7. Which management representative is responsible for the development of the plant's affirmative action program?

II. Recruitment

1. How are hourly employees recruited for this plant?

2. What do you consider to be the major problems confronting this plant with respect to the recruitment of:

   a. minorities?
   b. women?

III. Selection of Persons for Employment and Initial Placement

1. Describe the step-by-step procedure that is followed when a potential hourly employee applies for a job and is accepted or rejected.

2. What specific policies and/or written guidelines govern the selection process?

   (a. Job specifications; b. criteria for employment; c. procedures for recording interviews; d. orientation regarding the rest of the processing procedures.)

3. Are there any safeguards to prevent discrimination?

   ———Yes   ———No

   If yes, please specify.

4. Are tests required for entry-level positions?

   ———Yes   ———No

   If yes, What types of tests are administered?

5. Have these tests been validated locally?

   ———Yes   ———No

6. What is the relationship between test scores and employment opportunities?

7. Is the applicant given a tour of the operation and provided an opportunity to see the job(s) for which he or she is being considered?   ———Yes   ———No

8. Who makes the final decision to hire?

9. What are the personal characteristics that are considered essential for employment at this plant? Answer on reverse side.

   Identify   Define   How determined

   _____

   _____

   _____

   _____

   _____

10. What input provided in the employment process contributes most to your hiring decision: application form, test results, interview findings, etc.? Please rank these items in order of importance.

11. Do you see a need for changes in the employment selection process?   ———Yes   ———No

    If yes, What changes would you recommend?

IV. New Employee Orientation

1. Is there a new employee-orientation program?
   ____Yes ____No
   If yes, Are there written guidelines or procedures governing this program? ____Yes ____No

2. Who conducts this program and where?

3. What is the duration of this program?

4. What subjects are covered in this program?

V. Probationary Period

1. Is there a probationary period for new employees?
   ____Yes ____No
   If yes, How long is it?

2. Is the new employee informed about the probationary period and its requirements? ____Yes ____No
   If yes, When?

      How?

3. Are there formal guidelines governing the evaluation of new employees during the probationary period?
   ____Yes ____No

4. Who performs the evaluation of probationary employees?

5. How frequently during the probationary period are new employees evaluated?

6. What criteria are used in the evaluation of probationary employees? How much weight is given to each factor?

7. Are there any forms used to assist in probationary employee evaluations? ____Yes ____No
   If yes, please obtain copies.

VI. Training

1. Does this plant have a formal training policy?
   ____Yes ____No
   If yes, please describe.

2. What are the specific objectives of the plant's effort?

3. Are these objectives communicated to employees?
   _____Yes _____No
   If yes, How?

4. What actions have been undertaken to accomplish the plant's training objectives?

5. Who performs the plant's training?

6. What facilities and aids are provided to support the plant's training efforts: classrooms, audio/visual aids, manuals, etc.?

7. Approximately what percent of the plant's total training effort for hourly employees is accomplished through the following methods?
   a. on-the-job   _____%
   b. classroom   _____%
   c. educational institutions
      (colleges, technical schools, etc.)   _____%
   d. correspondence courses   _____%
   e. other(s) (please specify)   _____%

8. Are employees counselled as to:
   a. What training opportunities are available?
   _____Yes _____No
   If yes, How?

   b. How available training programs may affect their upward mobility? _____Yes _____No
   If yes, How?

9. How are hourly workers selected for the following training programs:
   a. technical skills and knowledge?
   b. supervisory skills and knowledge?

10. In what areas do hourly employees receive training?

11. Is there a direct relationship between training and promotion:
    a. to higher hourly jobs? _____Yes _____No
    If yes, please describe.

    b. to first-level supervisory jobs? _____Yes _____No
    If yes, please describe.

12. Do you see a need for any changes in the plant's current training effort? _____Yes _____No
    If yes, please specify.

VII. Transfers

1. Are there any plant policies and/or guidelines governing employee transfers?   ——Yes   ——No
   If yes, please describe.

2. Are there any restrictions imposed on transfers: frequency, between departments, divisions, etc.?
   ——Yes   ——No
   If yes, please identify.

3. Are transfer opportunities communicated to all employees?
   ——Yes   ——No
   If yes, How?

4. Who is involved in the transfer process and who must approve transfers?

5. What are the criteria for accepting or rejecting transfer requests?

6. Are these criteria written down?   ——Yes   ——No
   If yes, Who has access to them?

7. How is an employee requesting transfer evaluated against these criteria?

8. Is an employee informed if he or she has been rejected for a transfer and why?   ——Yes   ——No

9. Do you believe that this plant's transfer procedures present barriers to employee mobility?   ——Yes   ——No
   If yes, please explain.

10. Do you see a need for change in the plant's transfer procedures?   ——Yes   ——No
    If yes, What would you recommend?

VIII. Promotions (Nonsupervisory)

1. Are there policies and/or written guidelines governing promotion within this plant?   ——Yes   ——No
   If yes, please describe or obtain a copy.

2. Are there any restrictions imposed on promotions?
   ——Yes   ——No
   If yes, please identify.

3. Are there any safeguards to prevent discrimination and/or the possibility of overlooking qualified employees?
   ____Yes   ____No
   If yes, please specify.

4. Are there any employees for whom promotion possibilities seem very limited?   ____Yes   ____No
   If yes, please explain.

5. Are promotion opportunities communicated to all hourly employees?   ____Yes   ____No
   If yes, How?

6. Who is involved in selecting hourly employees for promotion and who makes the final determination?

7. Under what circumstances would the most senior man not be selected for promotion?

8. Is there an appraisal program for review and evaluation of an employee's job performance and potential for promotion?
   ____Yes   ____No
   If yes, please describe.

9. Are there any mechanisms set up to train employees for promotions?   ____Yes   ____No
   If yes, please describe.

10. Is an employee informed if he or she has not been accepted for promotion?   ____Yes   ____No
    If yes, How?

11. Do you see a need for change in the plant's promotion procedures?   ____Yes   ____No
    If yes, What would you recommend?

IX. Supervisor Selection

1. Are there any policies and/or written guidelines governing the selection of persons for first-level supervisor?
   ____Yes   ____No
   If yes, please describe or obtain a copy.

   To whom are these communicated?

2. Who is involved in selecting first-level supervisors and what is the extent of their involvement?

3. What are the personal characteristics that you consider essential for first-level supervisors?

   Identify   Define

   _____

   _____

   _____

   _____

   _____

4. Is there an appraisal program for review and evaluation of an employee's job performance and potential for promotion to first-level supervisor?   ____Yes   ____No
   If yes, please describe.

5. Are the factors considered important for promotion to first-level supervisor communicated to employees?
   ____Yes   ____No
   If yes, How?

6. What groups within the plant seem to have difficulty being promoted to first-level supervisor: race, sex, age, etc.?

7. How would you describe opportunities for promotion from an hourly position to a supervisory position within this plant? Why?

8. Are there any safeguards to prevent discrimination and/or the possibility of overlooking qualified employees for first-level supervisor?   ____Yes   ____No

9. Are employees informed that they are being considered for promotion to first-level supervisor?   ____Yes   ____No
   If yes, How?

       How are the unsuccessful employees informed as to why they were not selected?

10. Are there any mechanisms set up to train employees for promotion to first-level supervisor?   ____Yes   ____No
    If yes, please describe.

11. How important is it for persons being considered for first-level supervisory positions to have experience as relief supervisor or leadman?

12. What is the single most important element in the promotion process: supervisor's recommendation, seniority, test scores, etc.?

13. Do you maintain a roster of personnel eligible for promotion to foreman? _____Yes _____No
If yes, How is it developed and maintained?

14. Are hourly employees notified of promotion opportunities?
_____Yes _____No
If yes, How?

X. Summary

1. What specific barriers do you believe might prevent or hinder the upward movement of employees in this plant?

2. What do you suggest be done to reduce or eliminate these barriers?

APPENDIX B

Plant Manager Interview Form

1. Have you established formal objectives and/or guidelines for this plant with respect to:
   a. recruitment? ———Yes ———No
   b. hiring? ———Yes ———No
   c. new employee orientation? ———Yes ———No
   d. probationary period? ———Yes ———No
   e. placement? ———Yes ———No
   f. transfers? ———Yes ———No
   g. training? ———Yes ———No
   h. hourly promotions? ———Yes ———No
   i. selection of first-level supervisors? ———Yes ———No
   j. affirmative action programs? . ———Yes ———No

   If yes, briefly describe these goals and/or objectives.

   To whom are they communicated and how?

   If no, Who establishes such objectives and/or guidelines?

2. Is there any type of check or audit to insure that the policies and/or guidelines are being followed? ———Yes ———No
   If yes, please describe.

3. Are you directly involved in any of the ten activities named earlier? (Emphasize h, i, and j.) ———Yes ———No
   If yes, please describe your involvement.

4. Do you believe that there are any barriers, individual, organizational, or environmental, that might prevent or hinder the upward movement of employees in this plant? ———Yes ———No
   If yes, please describe.

5. What are the personal characteristics you consider essential for a first-level supervisor?

   Identify   Define

   _____

   _____

   _____

   _____

   _____

APPENDIX C

Departmental Interview Form

I. General

1. Has this department experienced any major hirings or layoffs during the last five years?   ——Yes   ——No
   If yes, please explain the causes for these changes.

2. In the last five years, have any of the following problem areas become more serious?
   a. absenteeism   ——Yes   ——No
   b. race relations   ——Yes   ——No
   c. discipline   ——Yes   ——No
   d. youth   ——Yes   ——No
   e. tardiness   ——Yes   ——No
   f. turnover   ——Yes   ——No
   g. morale   ——Yes   ——No

3. Are you involved personally in this plant's affirmative action program?   ——Yes   ——No
   If yes, What is your involvement?

II. Selection of Persons for Employment and Initial Placement

1. Is anyone in your department directly involved in the hiring of hourly employees?   ——Yes   ——No
   If yes, Who?

   Describe their involvement.

2. What written instructions and/or tools are available to guide them?

3. What training have they received in the selection of hourly employees?

III. New Employee Orientation

1. Does your department conduct an orientation program for new employees?   ——Yes   ——No
   If yes, Who is involved?

   Describe their involvement.

2. What subjects do they cover?

3. What written guidelines or procedures govern this program?

4. How long does the program last?

IV. Probationary Period

1. In your department, is there a probationary period for new employees? ____ Yes ____ No
   If yes, How long is it?

2. Who is involved?

   Describe their involvement.

3. How are employees informed of this program?

4. How frequently are employees evaluated?

5. What formal guidelines and/or forms assist in this effort?

V. Training

1. Does your own department have or participate in any training programs? ____ Yes ____ No
   If yes, What kind of program?

2. Who is involved in conducting the training?

   Describe their involvement.

3. What facilities and/or aids are used in the training programs?

4. How do employees learn of training programs?

5. How are employees selected for training?

6. What is the relationship between training and promotion?

7. How do employees learn of the effect training will have on their promotion possibilities?

VI. Transfers

1. Can an employee transfer in or out of this department?
   ____ Yes ____ No
   If yes, please describe the procedures.

2. Who is involved in the transfer process?

   Describe their involvement.

3. What restrictions are imposed?

4. How do employees learn of transfer opportunities?

5. What criteria are used by this department for accepting or rejecting transfer requests?

6. How is an employee informed if he has been accepted or rejected?

VII. Promotions (Nonsupervisory)

1. Are there policies and/or written guidelines governing promotions within this department? _____ Yes _____ No
   If yes, please describe or obtain a copy.

2. Are there any safeguards to prevent discrimination and/or overlooking qualified employees? _____ Yes _____ No
   If yes, please describe.

3. Are there any employees for whom promotion possibilities seem very limited? _____ Yes _____ No
   If yes, please explain.

4. How are promotion opportunities communicated to all employees?

5. Who is involved in promoting employees into higher hourly jobs, and what is their involvement?

6. Is the most senior man usually the person that is promoted? _____ Yes _____ No
   If yes, Under what circumstances would the most senior man not be selected for promotion?

7. Is there an appraisal program for the review and evaluation of an employee's job performance and/or potential for promotion? _____ Yes _____ No
   If yes, please describe. Obtain a copy of any formal procedures or forms used in this process.

8. How are employees trained to fill higher jobs?

9. Is an employee informed if he has not been accepted for promotion? _____ Yes _____ No
   If yes, How?

   Is he told why he was not accepted?

10. How would you describe the opportunities for promotion to higher hourly jobs within this department? Why?

VIII. Supervisor Selection

1. Are there any policies and/or written guidelines governing the selection of persons for first-level supervisor?
   ____ Yes ____ No

   If yes, please describe or obtain a copy.

2. Who is involved in the selection process and what is their involvement?

3. What are the personal characteristics that you consider important when you are asked to recommend or select someone for a position as a first-level supervisor?

   Identify   Define

   _____

   _____

   _____

   _____

   _____

4. When you ask your first-level supervisors for recommendations as to who should be considered for promotion to first-level supervisor, how do they know what characteristics or other criteria you desire in first-level supervisors?

5. Is there a formal appraisal program for reviewing and evaluating an employee's job performance and potential for promotion to first-level supervisor?   ____ Yes   ____ No

   If yes, please describe. Obtain a copy of any written information, forms, etc., that are used.

6. Are the factors considered important for promotion to first-level supervisor communicated to employees?
   ____ Yes   ____ No

   If yes, How?

7. What groups within this department seem to have difficulty being promoted to first-level supervisor: race, sex, age, etc.?

8. How would you describe opportunities for promotion from an hourly to a supervisory position within this department? Why?

9. Are employees informed that they are being considered for promotion to first-level supervisor?

_____ Yes   _____ No

If yes, How are they informed?

How are the unsuccessful employees informed as to why they were not selected?

10. What mechanisms are set up to train employees for promotion to first-level supervisors?

11. How important is it for persons being considered for first-level supervisory positions to have experience as relief supervisor or leadman?

12. What is the single most important element in the promotion process: supervisor's recommendation, seniority, test scores, etc.?

13. Are there any safeguards to prevent discrimination and/or overlooking qualified employees?   _____ Yes   _____ No

If yes, please describe.

14. Do you maintain a roster of department or plant personnel eligible for promotion to foreman?   _____ Yes   _____ No

If yes, How is it developed and maintained?

IX. Summary

1. Do you see a way that any of the personnel practices that we have just discussed could be improved?

_____ Yes   _____ No

If yes, How?

2. In your opinion, what are the major barriers or constraints that tend to prevent employees from moving into higher level jobs within this department?

APPENDIX D

*First-Line Supervisor
Interview Form*

1. Are you directly involved in the following employment practices?
   a. hiring   ____Yes   ____No
   b. new employee orientation   ____Yes   ____No
   c. initial job placement   ____Yes   ____No
   d. probationary period evaluations   ____Yes   ____No
   e. transfers   ____Yes   ____No
   f. training or selection of employees
   for training   ____Yes   ____No
   g. promotions to higher hourly jobs   ____Yes   ____No
   h. promotions of hourly employees to
   first-line supervisors   ____Yes   ____No
   If yes, please describe your involvement.

2. How would you describe the opportunities for promotion to higher hourly jobs within this department? Why?

3. Are there any major obstacles to promotion to higher hourly jobs?
   ____Yes   ____No
   If yes, please identify.

4. How would you describe the opportunities for promotion from an hourly job to a supervisory position within this department? Why?

5. Are there any major obstacles to promotion to a supervisory position?   ____Yes   ____No
   If yes, please identify.

6. Are you presently preparing one or more employees for the job of relief foreman, leadman, etc.?   ____Yes   ____No
   If yes, How many?

   What is their current position?

   Please describe what you do to prepare employees.

7. Have you ever had an employee tell you that he was not interested in a promotion to a higher hourly job?   ____Yes   ____No
   If yes, How often does this occur?

   What were their reasons?

8. Have you ever known of an employee rejecting an offer for promotion to first-level supervisor?   ____Yes   ____No
   If yes, How many?

   What were their reasons?

9. Do you have written instructions to aid you in selecting people for promotion to either higher hourly jobs or supervisory jobs?
_____Yes _____No
If yes, please describe or obtain a copy.

10. When you are asked to recommend employees for promotion to first-level supervisor, what personal characteristics do you consider?

Identify   Define

_____

_____

_____

_____

_____

11. What part of your job takes up the most time? Second most?

12. Why did you accept the offer to become a supervisor?

13. If you had the opportunity to make the decision over again, now that you know what it is like to be a supervisor, would you again accept the offer? _____Yes _____No
Why or why not?

14. What are the things you like most about being a supervisor?

15. What are the things you like least about being a supervisor?

16. Have you ever been a union officer? _____Yes _____No
If yes, What was your position?

Race of Interviewee: _____white
_____black
_____other

APPENDIX E

*Personal Data Collection Form
and Legend*

Figure E-1
Personal Data Collection Form

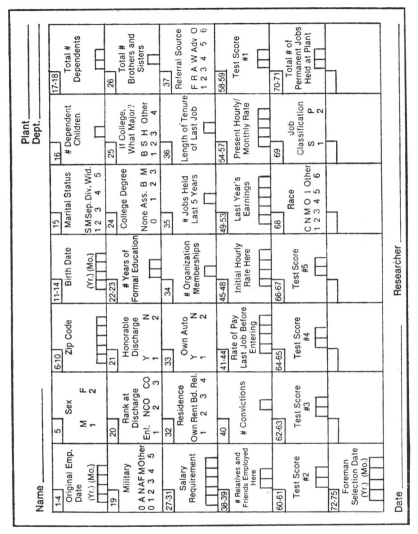

PERSONAL DATA COLLECTION FORM LEGEND

I. Instructions for Filling Out Form

1. Circle all numbers.   E.g.,   M   F
                                           1   2

2. Right justify all boxes.   E.g.,   Salary requirement
                                         \$8,500 = | 8 | 5 | 0 | 0 |

3. All dates are to include year-month only.
                       E.g.,   730327 = | 7 | 3 | 0 | 3 |

4. If question is not applicable, leave blank.

5. If foreman, list all jobs on reverse side of form and give date for permanent promotion to first-level supervisor.

II. Category Description

   #

1-4   Original employment date.   E.g., | 7 | 3 | 0 | 1 |

5   M̲ale   F̲emale

6-10   Zip code of home address (if not known: 99999 = city; 11111 = noncity).

11-14   Birth date.   E.g., | 4 | 6 | 1 | 0 |

15   S̲ingle, M̲arried, S̲eparated, D̲ivorced, W̲idowed.

16   If greater than 9, use | 9 | *

17-18   Indicate total number of dependents including children.

19   Military Service. If none, circle: ∅.
         A̲rmy, N̲avy, A̲ir F̲orce, M̲arines, O̲ther (e.g., Coast Guard).

20   Rank at time of discharge, determine best category: Enl. = enlisted; NCO = noncommissioned officer; CO = officer.

21   Yes, No.

22-23   E.g., thru College = | 1 | 6 |

24   N̲one, A̲ssociate, B̲achelor, M̲aster.

25   B̲usiness, S̲cience, H̲umanities, O̲ther.

26   Total number of brothers and sisters (if greater than 9, use | 9 | *).

27-31   Dollar figure only.   E.g., \$8,500 = | | 8 | 5 | 0 | 0 |

32   Residence? Own   Rent   Board   Relatives
                     1   2   3   4

33   Own your own automobile? Yes = 1   No = 2

34   E.g., Clubs, Societies, Community Groups.

35   If greater than 9, use | 9 | *

36   If greater than 9, use | 9 | *

37   F̲riend, R̲elative, A̲gency, W̲alk-in, A̲dvertisement, O̲ther.

38-39   E.g., 3 = | | 3 |

40   Number of criminal convictions for major offenses.

41-44   Dollar-cents figure. E.g., \$4.75 = [| 4 | 7 | 5]
45-48   Dollar-cents figure. E.g., \$12.00 = [1 | 2 | 0 | 0]
49-53   Dollar figure. E.g., \$14,500 = [1 | 4 | 5 | 0 | 0]
54-57   Dollar-cents figure. E.g., \$5.95 = [| 5 | 9 | 5]
        Circle "Hourly" or "Monthly" as is appropriate.
58-59   If 100, use [9 | 9] *
60-61   If 100, use [9 | 9] *
62-63   If 100, use [9 | 9] *
64-65   If 100, use [9 | 9] *
66-67   If 100, use [9 | 9] *

68   Caucasian, Negro, Mexican, Oriental, Indian, Other.
69   Supervisor (or Foreman), Production Worker.
70-71   For supervisors, do not bother to record until later, as this will be reflected in I, 5.
72-75   If employee is a foreman, give the date on which he became a permanent foreman.

APPENDIX F

Typical Descriptive Scale
Typical Characteristic-Ranking Form
Supervisor Selection Criteria for Sample
Industries

TYPICAL DESCRIPTIVE SCALE

Plant: _____

Your Name: _____

Your Title: _____

Your Department: _____

Date: _____

Name of Employee Under Consideration: _____

Instructions

This form lists some characteristics that are often used to describe employees. Following each characteristic, there is a statement that briefly defines the characteristic. This statement is designed to help overcome the possibility of different people having contrasting definitions for the same characteristic.

After you have read a characteristic and the accompanying statement, please answer the multiple choice question immediately following the statement. Your response should indicate how you feel the characteristic describes the employee under consideration. Your answers to these questions will help us develop a picture of this plant's work force.

It should be pointed out that the employee you are describing has been chosen on a random basis by our research team, as have all employees being considered in this exercise. In addition, the information you are providing us is completely confidential and will in no way affect the status of the employees under consideration. After you have finished with this form, give it to your supervisor. He will see to it that it is returned to us.

Thank you very much for your assistance.

I. Leadership

This characteristic describes someone who has the ability to lead and to motivate others, commands respect from his fellow workers, can delegate work effectively, and is the type of person that people will seek out for help.

For the employee under consideration, this characteristic is

1. _____ highly descriptive.
2. _____ considerably descriptive.
3. _____ moderately descriptive.
4. _____ slightly descriptive.
5. _____ not descriptive at all.

II. Attitude/Loyalty

This characteristic describes someone who is interested in the company, is eager to please the company, is interested in his work and his job, and takes pride in his work.

For the employee under consideration, this characteristic is

1. _____ highly descriptive.
2. _____ considerably descriptive.
3. _____ moderately descriptive.
4. _____ slightly descriptive.
5. _____ not descriptive at all.

III. Job Knowledge

This characteristic describes someone who knows his own job or trade very well, knows the production process, has a considerable amount of job experience, is a fairly good mechanic, and can teach others about the job if necessary.

For the employee under consideration, this characteristic is

1. _____ highly descriptive.
2. _____ considerably descriptive.
3. _____ moderately descriptive.
4. _____ slightly descriptive.
5. _____ not descriptive at all.

IV. Dependability/Responsibility

This characteristic describes someone who is a good worker, works with you and not against you, can always be depended upon to do a good job, and is a very responsible person.

For the employee under consideration, this characteristic is

1. _____ highly descriptive.
2. _____ considerably descriptive.
3. _____ moderately descriptive.
4. _____ slightly descriptive.
5. _____ not descriptive at all.

V. Ability to Get Along with People

This characteristic describes someone who has a good relationship with the people with whom he works, has a good personality, can get along with contractors as well as supervisors and hourly employees, and treats people as he would like to be treated.

For the employee under consideration, this characteristic is

1. _____ highly descriptive.
2. _____ considerably descriptive.
3. _____ moderately descriptive.
4. _____ slightly descriptive.
5. _____ not descriptive at all.

VI. Common Sense

This characteristic describes someone who is logical and can analyze most situations, can handle upsets, and shows good common sense.

For the employee under consideration, this characteristic is

1. _____ highly descriptive.
2. _____ considerably descriptive.
3. _____ moderately descriptive.
4. _____ slightly descriptive.
5. _____ not descriptive at all.

TYPICAL CHARACTERISTIC-RANKING FORM

Job Title: _____

Department: _____

Instructions

Below is a list of characteristics that are often used to evaluate an employee's potential as a first-level supervisor. Based on your personal judgment, rank these characteristics in order of their importance. For example, the characteristic that you consider to be the *most* important for a first-level supervisor to possess should be assigned the number "1," the second most important a "2," and so on for all characteristics listed.

1. Leadership

This characteristic describes someone who has the ability to lead and to motivate others, commands respect from his fellow workers, can delegate work effectively, and is the type of person that people will seek out for help.

2. Attitude/Loyalty

This characteristic describes someone who is interested in the company, is eager to please the company, is interested in his work and his job, and takes pride in his work.

3. Job Knowledge

This characteristic describes someone who knows his own job or trade very well, knows the production process, has a considerable amount of job experience, is a fairly good mechanic, and can teach others about the job if necessary.

4. Dependability/Responsibility

This characteristic describes someone who is a good worker, works with you and not against you, can always be depended upon to do a good job, and is a very responsible person.

5. Ability to Get Along with People

This characteristic describes someone who has a good relationship with the people with whom he works, has a good personality, can get along with contractors as well as supervisors and hourly employees, and treats people as he would like to be treated.

6. Common Sense

This characteristic describes someone who is logical and can analyze most situations, can handle upsets, and shows good common sense.

AIRCRAFT MANUFACTURER
MAJOR SUPERVISOR SELECTION CRITERIA

1. Ability to Get Along with People

This characteristic describes someone who gets along with his fellow workers and his supervisors, has a good personality, is tactful, treats people as he would like to be treated, and is cooperative.

2. Initiative

This characteristic describes someone who is ambitious, has desire and drive, wants to get ahead, is aggressive, is highly motivated, and has a self-starting ability.

3. Job Knowledge/Technical Ability

This characteristic describes someone who has the necessary technical skills, knows the job and is mechanically able to do the job, and knows and understands blueprints.

4. Attitude

This characteristic describes someone who is loyal to the company, has a good attitude toward the company and his job, is interested in his job, is willing to spend extra time on the job if necessary, and has high morale.

5. Good Work Record

This characteristic describes someone who is a good worker, is conscientious on the job, has good work habits, follows through on his job, accepts responsibility, is dependable, has a good attendance record, and is almost always on time for work.

TABLE F-1
Aircraft Manufacturer
Ranking of Supervisor Selection Criteria

Assistant Foremen (N = 38)		Foremen (N = 36)	
Criterion	Average Ranking	Criterion	Average Ranking
Attitude	2.3	Initiative	1.7
Initiative	2.4	Attitude	2.7
Ability to get along with people	2.8	Ability to get along with people	2.7
Good work record	3.4	Good work record	3.9
Job knowledge, technical ability	3.6	Job knowledge, technical ability	4.0

General Foremen (N = 16)		Superintendents (N = 16)	
Criterion	Average Ranking	Criterion	Average Ranking
Initiative	1.9	Initiative	2.2
Attitude	2.4	Ability to get along with people	2.6
Ability to get along with people	2.9	Job knowledge, technical ability	3.2
Good work record	3.9	Attitude	3.5
Job knowledge, technical ability	3.9	Good work record	3.6

CHEMICAL MANUFACTURER
MAJOR SUPERVISOR SELECTION CRITERIA

1. Leadership

This characteristic describes someone who has demonstrated leadership potential in the past, is looked up to in a group as an informal leader, can delegate responsibilities, and can take charge of a situation when necessary.

2. Dependability/Reliability

This characteristic describes someone who can be depended on to do a good job, has a good absentee record, is rarely late for work, obeys regulations, and, in general, is a responsible person.

3. Intelligence

This characteristic describes someone who is reasonably intelligent, has enough education to read and be able to account for things, and is able to follow instructions.

4. Mechanical Aptitude/Job Knowledge

This characteristic describes someone who is mechanically inclined, has a reasonably high level of job experience, knows his job well, and has a good overall knowledge of the plant.

5. Cooperative

This characteristic describes someone who is reasonable in his dealings with others, is not always out for his own self-interest, and is not frequently creating problems with his fellow employees.

6. Job Performance

This characteristic describes someone who has a good work record, does a good job, commits few operating errors, keeps his operation or building running well, and gets the work done.

7. Ability to Get Along with People

This characteristic describes someone who has a good personality, is tactful in dealing with other people, is well thought of by his fellow workers, is able to put himself in another's place, and understands and gets along with various types of people.

8. Initiative

This characteristic describes someone who is ambitious, wants to better himself, has a desire for advancement, accepts a challenge, is highly motivated, and is enthusiastic about his own job.

ELECTRICAL PRODUCTS MANUFACTURER
MAJOR SUPERVISOR SELECTION CRITERIA

1. Leadership

This characteristic describes someone who has the ability to lead others, can handle other people, has the ability and courage to make decisions, and can give and take orders.

2. Desire/Initiative

This characteristic describes someone who is aggresive, has a desire to get ahead, is motivated, has a good attitude toward his work, and is eager to do a good job.

3. Intelligence

This characteristic describes someone who has the ability to learn, has a sufficient level of education, shows common sense, can understand orders, and has the ability to reason out a problem.

TABLE F-2
Chemical Manufacturer
Ranking of Supervisor Selection Criteria

Foremen (N = 28)		Superintendents (N = 7)	
Criterion	Average Ranking	Criterion	Average Ranking
Leadership	1.7	Leadership	1.6
Intelligence	3.9	Initiative	3.3
Dependability, reliability	4.0	Intelligence	3.9
Mechanical aptitude, job knowledge	4.6	Dependability, reliability	4.6
Job performance	4.6	Ability to get along with people	5.3
Initiative	5.1	Job performance	5.4
Ability to get along with people	5.7	Cooperative	5.9
Cooperative	5.8	Mechanical aptitude, job knowledge	6.1

TABLE F-3
Electrical Products Manufacturer
Ranking of Supervisor Selection Criteria

Foremen and Supervisors (N = 20)		General Foremen (N = 4)	
Criterion	Average Ranking	Criterion	Average Ranking
Leadership	1.6	Leadership	1.2
Job knowledge	3.4	Job knowledge	2.0
Intelligence	3.6	Intelligence	4.0
Desire, initiative	3.8	Strong character	4.5
Ability to get along with people	5.0	Ability to get along with people	5.0
Dependability	5.0	Desire, initiative	5.2
Strong character	5.6	Dependability	6.0

4. **Job Knowledge**

This characteristic describes someone who has a good understanding of his job and the overall operations of the plant, knows the product, has mechanical abilities, and is able to trouble shoot when necessary.

5. **Ability to Get Along with People**

This characteristic describes someone who knows how to get along with others, works well with others, has a good relationship with other employees, is able to know how other people feel, and understands people and treats them as individuals.

6. **Dependability**

This characteristic describes someone who is reliable, has a good absentee record, is rarely late for work, and does not have to be double-checked frequently to make sure he is doing his job.

7. **Strong Character**

This characteristic describes someone who is or would be able to deal with the union, knows his own mind, is strong minded, has guts, can say no and make it stick, and has strong convictions.

FOOD PROCESSING PLANT
MAJOR SUPERVISOR SELECTION CRITERIA

1. **Initiative**

This characteristic describes someone who is motivated, has desire and drive, is aggressive, and is eager to get ahead.

2. **Job Knowledge**

This characteristic describes someone who has a general knowledge of the operation, knows his job, knows how to use the equipment, and understands the overall basic operations.

3. **Ability to Get Along with People**

This characteristic describes someone who is cooperative, has a good personality, and treats people as he would like to be treated.

4. **Leadership**

This characteristic describes someone who is able to handle people, is respected by his fellow workers, can make his own decisions, can get the job done through others, is able to organize his work, and can motivate others.

5. Dedication

This characteristic describes someone who is committed to the company, the plant and his job, takes pride in his job, likes his work, does what he is told, and is willing to do a little extra in order to do a better job.

6. Education/Intelligence

This characteristic describes someone who is intelligent enough to do the job, has enough formal schooling to perform the administrative aspects of the job, and is of at least average intelligence.

7. Job Performance

This characteristic describes someone who is reliable and conscientious, is willing to work until the job is done, is willing to work overtime or on Saturdays when necessary, does not let up when the supervisor is away, and does not require constant supervision.

PAPER MANUFACTURER
MAJOR SUPERVISOR SELECTION CRITERIA

1. Good Health

This characteristic describes someone who is physically fit, has no serious physical impairments, misses little work time because of health problems, and is emotionally stable.

2. Attitude

This characteristic describes someone who does his job well, is enthusiastic about his job, is interested in his job and his department, and is loyal to the company and to his superiors.

3. Initiative

This characteristic describes someone who has the desire to get ahead, is willing to do things on his own without always having to be told to do them, has the drive to get the job done, and is interested in upgrading or improving himself on and off the job.

4. Leadership

This characteristic describes someone who can make decisions, is willing to take on responsibility, can motivate others so that the work gets done, and takes the lead in dealing with problems.

5. Job Knowledge

This characteristic describes someone who has a good knowledge of the machinery and the general production process, knows how to do his job well, is experienced in doing the work, and is technically competent.

TABLE F-4
Food Processing Plant
Ranking of Supervisor Selection Criteria

Supervisors		Area Managers		Managers	
Criterion	Average Ranking	Criterion	Average Ranking	Criterion	Average Ranking
Leadership	2.4	Leadership	1.0	Leadership	2.1
Job performance	3.6	Initiative	3.6	Initiative	3.6
Job knowledge	3.6	Job performance	3.7	Job knowledge	3.6
Initiative	3.8	Dedication	4.4	Education, intelligence	4.0
Dedication	4.1	Education, intelligence	4.7	Job performance	4.2
Ability to get along with people	4.4	Job knowledge	5.0	Dedication	5.0
Education, intelligence	4.9	Ability to get along with people	5.7	Ability to get along with people	5.4

TABLE F-5
Paper Manufacturer
Ranking of Supervisor Selection Criteria

Foremen (N = 25)		Superintendents (N = 20)	
Criterion	Average Ranking	Criterion	Average Ranking
Leadership	2.4	Leadership	2.6
Good health	3.8	Initiative	3.0
Attitude	3.8	Attitude	3.8
Job knowledge	4.0	Ability to get along with people	4.2
Ability to get along with people	4.0	Job knowledge	4.4
Initiative	4.0	Fairness	4.9
Fairness	5.9	Good health	5.3

6. Ability to Get Along with People

This characteristic describes someone who has a good personality, can get the job done without irritating people, gets along with people both above and below him, understands different types of people, and can control his temper.

7. Fairness

This characteristic describes someone who is not prejudiced, treats all people the same, is just in dealing with others, weighs both sides of an issue before making a decision, and is impartial.

PETROLEUM REFINERY
MAJOR SUPERVISOR SELECTION CRITERIA

1. Leadership

This characteristic describes someone who has the ability to lead and to motivate others, commands respect from his fellow workers, can delegate work effectively, and is the type of person that people will seek out for help.

2. Attitude/Loyalty

This characteristic describes someone who is interested in the company, is eager to please the company, is interested in his work and his job, and takes pride in his work.

3. Job Knowledge

This characteristic describes someone who knows his own job or trade very well, knows the production process, has a considerable amount of job experience, is a fairly good mechanic, and can teach others about the job if necessary.

4. Dependability/Responsibility

This characteristic describes someone who is a good worker, works with you and not against you, can always be depended upon to do a good job, and is a very responsible person.

5. Ability to Get Along with People

This characteristic describes someone who has a good relationship with the people with whom he works, has a good personality, can get along with contractors as well as supervisors and hourly employees, and treats people as he would like to be treated.

6. Common Sense

This characteristic describes someone who is logical and can analyze most situations, can handle upsets, and shows good common sense.

TABLE F-6
Petroleum Refinery
Ranking of Supervisor Selection Criteria

Foremen (N = 35)	Average Ranking
Criterion	
Leadership	2.3
Job knowledge	3.1
Dependability, responsibility	3.5
Common sense	3.7
Ability to get along with people	3.9
Attitude, loyalty	4.5

Supervisors (N = 11)	Average Ranking
Criterion	
Leadership	3.0
Attitude, loyalty	3.0
Job knowledge	3.4
Common sense	3.5
Dependability, responsibility	3.9
Ability to get along with people	4.2

General Foremen (N = 12)	Average Ranking
Criterion	
Leadership	2.4
Dependability, responsibility	3.2
Common sense	3.5
Attitude, loyalty	3.8
Job knowledge	3.8
Ability to get along with people	4.2

Superintendents (N = 8)	Average Ranking
Criterion	
Leadership	1.9
Common sense	3.2
Job knowledge	3.4
Dependability, responsibility	3.5
Ability to get along with people	4.0
Attitude, loyalty	5.0

Directors (N = 14)	Average Ranking
Criterion	
Leadership	1.8
Job knowledge	3.0
Common sense	3.7
Dependability, responsibility	3.9
Ability to get along with people	3.9
Attitude, loyalty	4.7

Personnel (N = 4)	Average Ranking
Criterion	
Leadership	1.0
Ability to get along with people	2.5
Attitude, loyalty	3.5
Dependability, responsibility	4.5
Job knowledge	4.8
Common sense	4.8

APPENDIX G

Quantifiable Personal Data

TABLE G-1
Aircraft Manufacturer
Quantifiable Personal Data

Variable	First-Line Supervisors vs. Hourly Employees						
	Means		Standard Deviation		Sample Size		Z
	S	H	S	H	S	H	
Current Age	44.26	45.77	7.56	9.54	196	292	1.94
Current Seniority	18.93	17.85	4.79	7.27	196	294	1.98[a]
Number of Experience Areas in the Plant	2.31	1.24	1.76	1.50	196	294	7.00[b]
Age at Time of Plant Employment	25.33	27.89	6.32	6.80	196	292	4.25[b]
Years of Education	12.08	11.00	0.89	1.74	165	208	7.78[b]
Number of Company Training Programs	11.95	4.36	4.59	3.25	195	261	20.77[b]
Number of Noncompany Training Programs	1.41	1.00	0.78	—	22	11	3.08[b]
Number of Professional Licenses and Unique Skills	1.89	1.78	1.16	0.96	74	59	3.64[b]
Number of Professional Honor Societies	0.03	0.01	0.25	0.18	196	294	0.99
Number of Jobs Held in Last Five Years	0.62	0.35	0.92	0.75	196	294	3.43[b]
Length of Last Job	1.10	0.65	2.10	1.67	196	294	2.60[b]

Key: S = First-line supervisors.
H = Hourly employees.

[a]Significant at the 5 percent level (Z = 1.960).
[b]Significant at the 1 percent level (Z = 2.575).

TABLE G-2
Automobile Assembly Plant
Quantifiable Personal Data

| | First-Line Supervisors vs. Hourly Employees | | | | | | |
| | Means | | Standard Deviation | | Sample Size | | |
Variable	S	H	S	H	S	H	Z
Current Age	42.29	37.54	9.07	11.17	174	251	4.82[c]
Current Seniority	17.91	11.50	7.75	8.14	175	255	8.25[c]
Number of Permanent Jobs Held at the Plant	4.70[b]	3.63	3.31	3.09	175	258	3.39[c]
Age at Time of Plant Employment[a]	24.38	25.81	4.95	6.63	174	248	2.54[d]
Number of Dependent Children[a]	0.77	0.80	1.09	1.22	175	258	0.27
Total Number of Dependents[a]	1.43	2.03	1.40	1.61	175	258	4.11[c]
Years of Education[a]	11.62	10.99	1.59	1.88	173	253	3.72[c]
Number of Organization Memberships[a]	—	0.04	—	0.23	175	258	2.87[c]
Number of Jobs Held in Last Five Years[a]	2.09	1.86	1.22	1.10	175	258	2.00[d]
Length of Last Job[a]	1.79	2.09	1.79	2.27	175	258	1.53
Number of Relatives and Friends Employed Here[a]	0.31	0.48	0.62	0.78	175	258	2.52[d]
Number of Convictions[a]	—	0.01	—	0.11	175	258	1.61

Key: S = First-line supervisors.
     H = Hourly employees.

[a]These variables are as of the date of hire and do not represent current situations.

[b]This number does not include the position of first-line supervisor.

[c]Significant at the 1 percent level ($Z = 2.575$).

[d]Significant at the 5 percent level ($Z = 1.960$).

TABLE G-3
Chemical Manufacturer
Quantifiable Personal Data

| | First-Line Supervisors vs. Hourly Employees | | | | | | |
| | Means | | Standard Deviation | | Sample Size | | |
Variable	S	H	S	H	S	H	Z
Current Age	42.29	38.51	8.94	12.41	44	64	1.84
Current Seniority	17.78[b]	12.89	8.18	8.30	45	63	3.04[c]
Number of Permanent Jobs Held at the Plant	4.89[b]	4.38	3.27	1.98	45	65	0.93
Age at Time of Plant Employment[a]	24.70	26.07	5.81	7.12	44	62	1.09
Number of Dependent Children[a]	0.62	0.77	1.12	1.20	45	65	0.67
Total Number of Dependents[a]	1.02	0.77	1.77	1.42	45	65	0.79
Years of Education[a]	12.23	11.80	0.73	1.28	44	64	2.21[d]
Number of Brothers and Sisters[a]	0.24	—	1.14	—	45	65	1.41
Number of Organization Memberships[a]	0.31	0.14	0.69	0.46	45	65	1.44
Number of Jobs Held in Last Five Years[a]	1.76	1.69	1.25	1.19	45	65	0.29
Length of Last Job[a]	1.60	1.95	1.68	2.20	45	65	0.95
Number of Relatives and Friends Employed Here[a]	1.04	0.72	1.21	1.20	45	65	1.37
Test No. 1	19.96	21.38	6.22	4.85	24	8	0.67
Test No. 2	43.33	40.11	8.63	8.75	33	46	1.63
Test No. 3	18.45	16.69	5.05	4.56	33	48	1.60
Test No. 4	50.50	44.60	13.50	8.83	2	10	0.59

Key: S = First-line supervisors.
　　　H = Hourly employees.

[a]These variables are as of the date of hire and do not represent current situations.

[b]This number does not include the position of first-line supervisor.

[c]Significant at the 1 percent level ($Z = 2.575$).

[d]Significant at the 5 percent level ($Z = 1.960$).

TABLE G-4
Electrical Products Manufacturer
Quantifiable Personal Data

| | First-Line Supervisors vs. Hourly Employees | | | | | | |
| | Means | | Standard Deviation | | Sample Size | | Z |
Variable	S	H	S	H	S	H	
Current Age	43.17	45.56	9.97	13.99	25	125	1.02
Current Seniority	12.53	18.23	12.12	15.14	26	126	2.09[d]
Number of Permanent Jobs Held at the Plant	2.88[b]	8.43	3.30	7.65	26	126	5.91[c]
Age at Time of Plant Employment[a]	30.30	27.19	10.16	7.76	25	125	1.45
Number of Dependent Children[a]	1.69	0.83	1.61	1.25	26	126	2.56[d]
Years of Education[a]	13.28	10.86	1.69	1.81	25	111	6.40[c]
Number of Brothers and Sisters[a]	0.42	0.96	1.52	2.10	26	126	1.53
Number of Organization Memberships[a]	0.73	0.27	1.37	0.64	26	126	1.67
Number of Jobs Held in Last Five Years[a]	1.38	1.58	1.08	1.39	26	126	0.82
Length of Last Job[a]	3.08	2.06	3.57	2.75	26	126	1.37
Number of Relatives and Friends Employed Here[a]	0.19	0.44	0.48	0.71	26	126	2.21[d]

Key: S = First-line supervisors.
     H = Hourly employees.

[a] These variables are as of the date of hire and do not represent current situations.

[b] This number does not include the position of first-line supervisor.

[c] Significant at the 1 percent level ($Z = 2.575$).

[d] Significant at the 5 percent level ($Z = 1.960$).

TABLE G-5
Food Processing Plant
Quantifiable Personal Data

| | First-Line Supervisors vs. Hourly Employees | | | | | | |
| | Means | | Standard Deviation | | Sample Size | | |
Variable	S	H	S	H	S	H	Z
Current Age	36.85	35.17	7.91	11.73	48	154	1.13
Current Seniority	7.84	5.50	2.48	2.76	49	155	5.60[b]
Number of Permanent Jobs Held at the Plant	0.78	2.90	1.34	1.63	49	155	9.13[b]
Age at Time of Plant Employment[a]	29.05	29.66	7.35	10.79	48	154	0.44
Number of Dependent Children[a]	1.47	1.17	1.40	1.49	49	155	1.29
Years of Education[a]	13.04	10.99	1.59	1.91	49	154	7.47[b]
Number of Organization Memberships[a]	0.73	0.06	0.83	0.25	49	155	5.61[b]
Number of Jobs Held in Last Five Years[a]	1.92	1.51	0.99	1.12	49	155	2.46[c]
Length of Last Job[a]	3.73	1.83	3.14	2.62	49	155	3.83[b]
Number of Relatives and Friends Employed Here[a]	0.78	1.70	1.31	1.64	49	155	4.01[b]

Key: S = First-line supervisors.
     H = Hourly employees.

[a]These variables are as of the date of hire and do not represent current situations.
[b]Significant at the 1 percent level ($Z = 2.575$).
[c]Significant at the 5 percent level ($Z = 1.960$).

TABLE G-6
Nonferrous Smelter
Quantifiable Personal Data

| Variable | First-Line Supervisors vs. Hourly Employees | | | | | | |
| | Means | | Standard Deviation | | Sample Size | | Z |
	S	H	S	H	S	H	
Current Age	46.45	42.11	9.07	13.65	120	155	3.16[b]
Current Seniority	21.51	16.92	10.21	11.31	119	154	3.51[b]
Number of Permanent Jobs Held at the Plant	6.66	N.A.	4.65	N.A.	120	N.A.	N.A.
Age at Time of Plant Employment[a]	24.93	24.99	6.81	6.76	116	148	0.07
Number of Dependent Children[a]	1.13	1.00	1.40	1.45	120	155	0.75
Total Number of Dependents[a]	1.89	1.65	1.77	1.89	120	155	1.08
Years of Education[a]	11.71	11.03	1.91	1.79	118	149	2.96[b]
Number of Brothers and Sisters[a]	0.05	0.12	0.34	0.66	120	155	1.14
Number of Organization Memberships[a]	0.21	0.01	0.48	0.16	120	155	4.35[b]
Number of Jobs Held in Last Five Years[a]	1.47	2.10	1.32	1.45	120	155	3.77[b]
Length of Last Job[a]	1.52	1.40	2.20	1.78	120	155	0.49
Number of Relatives and Friends Employed Here[a]	0.30	0.85	0.63	1.09	120	155	5.28[b]

Key: S = First-line supervisors.
   H = Hourly employees.

[a]These variables are as of the date of hire and do not represent current situations.

[b]Significant at the 1 percent level ($Z = 2.575$).

N.A. Not available.

TABLE G-7
Paper Manufacturer
Quantifiable Personal Data

| | First-Line Supervisors vs. Hourly Employees | | | | | | |
| | Means | | Standard Deviation | | Sample Size | | |
Variable	S	H	S	H	S	H	Z
Current Age	52.51	42.05	7.06	11.57	77	226	9.39[b]
Current Seniority	29.99	17.95	5.71	9.42	77	228	13.36[b]
Number of Permanent Jobs Held at the Plant	9.08	4.11	3.77	2.31	77	228	10.89[b]
Age at Time of Plant Employment[a]	22.26	24.26	4.46	4.86	76	220	—
Number of Dependent Children[a]	1.40	0.91	1.28	1.23	77	228	2.93[b]
Total Number of Dependents[a]	2.69	1.96	1.65	1.61	77	228	3.38[b]
Years of Education[a]	10.29	9.75	2.13	2.72	75	224	1.77[c]
Number of Brothers and Sisters[a]	3.14	3.51	2.28	2.56	77	228	1.19
Number of Organization Memberships[a]	0.03	—	0.16	0.07	77	228	1.52
Number of Jobs Held in Last Five Years[a]	1.69	1.84	1.21	1.23	77	228	0.94
Length of Last Job[a]	2.23	1.27	2.10	1.65	77	228	3.65[b]
Number of Relatives and Friends Employed Here[a]	1.14	0.97	1.26	1.07	77	228	1.00
Number of Convictions[a]	—	0.05	—	0.22	77	228	1.51
Test No. 1[a]	54.75	44.92	31.18	25.52	57	24	1.48
Test No. 2[a]	61.63	61.14	20.00	26.43	24	182	0.11
Test No. 3[a]	60.38	54.04	27.78	27.17	56	180	1.54
Test No. 4	57.74	50.91	30.39	30.60	54	157	1.42

Key: S = First-line supervisors.
　　　H = Hourly employees.

[a]These variables are as of the date of hire and do not represent current situations.

[b]Significant at the 1 percent level ($Z = 2.575$).

[c]Significant at the 10 percent level ($Z = 1.645$).

TABLE G-8
Petroleum Refinery
Quantifiable Personal Data

| | First-Line Supervisors vs. Hourly Employees | | | | | | |
| | Means | | Standard Deviation | | Sample Size | | |
Variable	S	H	S	H	S	H	Z
Current Age	54.01	41.26	7.42	13.06	70	153	9.24[d]
Current Seniority	30.40	14.35	7.16[c]	11.57	72	154	12.78[d]
Number of Permanent Jobs Held at the Plant	6.15[b]	7.46	3.91	6.29	72	154	1.91
Age at Time of Plant Employment[a]	23.69	26.90	4.64	6.79	70	153	4.12[d]
Number of Dependent Children[a]	0.50	0.62	0.93	0.97	72	154	0.89
Years of Education[a]	11.87	11.64	2.53	1.25	71	148	0.72
Number of Organization Memberships[a]	0.47	0.24	0.83	0.72	72	154	2.02[d]
Number of Jobs Held in Last Five Years[a]	1.65	1.80	1.35	1.33	72	154	0.78
Length of Last Job[a]	1.57	2.54	2.04	2.65	72	154	3.02[d]
Number of Relatives and Friends Employed Here[a]	1.51	1.88	1.48	1.64	72	154	1.69

Key: S = First-line supervisors.
H = Hourly employees.

[a]These variables are as of the date of hire and do not represent current situations.

[b]This number does not include the position of first-line supervisor.

[c]Significant at the 5 percent level (Z = 1.960).

[d]Significant at the 1 percent level (Z = 2.575).

APPENDIX H

*A Partial Listing of Organizations
Using the Assessment
Center Method*

Agway Inc.
Aluminum Co. of Canada, Ltd.
American Airlines, Inc.
American Hospital Supply Corp.
American Telephone &
Telegraph Co.
Anglo American Corp. of
South Africa, Ltd.
Armco Steel Corp.
Baylor University
Bendix Corp.
Blue Cross Association
Blue Cross & Blue Shield of Illinois
British Columbia Hydro
Power Authority
British Columbia Telephone Co.
Brown & Williamson Tobacco Corp.
Campbell Ewald Co.
Central Telephone &
Utilities Corp.
Chevrolet Motor Division
Ciba-Geigy Corp.
Clark Equipment Co.
Consolidated Edison of
New York, Inc.
Consumers Power Co.
Continental Telephone Corporation
Control Data Corp.
Duke Power Co.
Federal Bureau of Investigation
First & Merchants National Bank
Forty Plus of Canada
General Cable Corp.
General Electric Co.
Gino's Inc.
Harrah's Tahoe
Harris Corporation—
Semiconductor Div.
Heil Co.
Hoffman-La Roche Inc.
Huyck Corp.
Internal Revenue Service
International Association of
Chiefs of Police, Inc.
International Business
Machines Corp.
S. C. Johnson & Son, Inc.
Kendall Co.

Knight-Ridder Newspapers, Inc.
Eli Lilly and Company (Germany)
Lincoln First Bank of Rochester
Lincoln Public Schools (Nebraska)
Mallinckrodt Inc.
Manitoba, Province of
Maryland National Bank
McGraw-Hill Book Co.
F. W. Means & Co.
Merrill Lynch, Pierce, Fenner &
Smith Incorporated
Motorola, Inc.
NCR Corp.
Nationwide Life Insurance Co.
New York City
Northern Electric Co.
Northern Illinois Gas Co.
Olin Corp.—Ecusta Paper Div.
Ortho Diagnostics Inc.
Ortho Pharmaceutical Corporation
Owens-Illinois, Inc.
J. C. Penney Company, Inc.
Pfizer Company Ltd. (Canada)
Procter & Gamble Co.
Prudential Insurance Co. of
America
Qantas Airways Ltd.
Questor Corp.
Rohm & Haas Company
Sandoz, Inc.—Dorsey Laboratories
Schering Corporation
Sears, Roebuck and Company
Shell Oil Co.
SmithKline Corp.
South African Mutual Life
Assurance Society
Standard Oil Co. (Ohio)
Stanford University
State Organization for
Administration and Employment
Affairs—Iran
Steinberg's Ltd.
USM Corporation
Union Planters National Bank
United States Agricultural
Marketing Service
United States Air Force
United States Army

United States Civil Service
   Commission
United States Office of Management
   and the Budget
United States Social Security
   Administration

University of Colorado
Upjohn Company
Virginia National Bank
The Wickes Corporation
Wisconsin, State of
York Graphics Services, Inc.

APPENDIX I

Selected List of Validity Studies
Sample Findings

Bentz, V. Jon. "Validity Studies at Sears." *Proceedings of the 79th Annual Convention of the American Psychological Association,* Vol. 6 (1971), p. 870. (Sears, Roebuck and Company.)

Bray, Douglas W., and Campbell, Richard J. "Selection of Salesmen by Means of an Assessment Center." *Journal of Applied Psychology,* Vol. 52 (February 1968), pp. 36-41. (American Telephone & Telegraph Company.)

Bullard, J. F. "An Evaluation of the Assessment Center Approach to Selecting Supervisors." Peoria, Ill.: Caterpillar Tractor Co., Corporate Personnel Department, May 1969.

Campbell, Richard J., and Bray, Douglas W. "Assessment Centers: An Aid in Management Selection." *Personnel Administration,* Vol. 30 (March-April 1967), pp. 7-13.

Carleton, Frederick O. "Relationships Between Follow-Up Evaluations and Information Developed in a Management Assessment Center." *Proceedings of the 78th Annual Convention of the American Psychological Association,* Vol. 5 (1970), pp. 565-66. (Standard Oil Company.)

Dodd, William E. "Validity Studies at IBM." *Proceedings of the 79th Annual Convention of the American Psychological Association,* Vol. 6 (1971), p. 870. (IBM Corporation.)

Finley, Robert, Jr. "Evaluation of Behavior Predictions from Projective Tests Given in a Management Assessment Center." *Proceedings of the 78th Annual Convention of the American Psychological Association,* Vol. 5 (1970), pp. 567-68. (Standard Oil Company.)

Ginsburg, Lee R., and Silverman, Arnold. "The Leaders of Tomorrow: Their Identification and Development." *Personnel Journal,* Vol. 51 (September 1972), pp. 662-66.

Hinrichs, John R. "A Cross-National Evaluation of Assessment Centers in Eight Countries." *Assessment and Development,* Vol. 2 (January 1975), pp. 1 and 5.

Jaffee, Cabot L.; Cohen, Stephen L.; and Cherry, Robert. "Supervisory Selection Program for Disadvantaged or Minority Employees." *Training and Development Journal,* Vol. 26 (January 1972), pp. 22-27.

Kraut, Allen I., and Scott, Grant J. "Validity of an Operational Management Assessment Program." *Journal of Applied Psychology,* Vol. 56 (April 1972), pp. 124-29. (IBM Corporation.)

McConnell, John J., and Parker, Treadway C. "An Assessment Center Program for Multi-Organizational Use." *Training and Development Journal,* Vol. 26 (March 1972), pp. 6-14. (American Management Association, Inc.)

Mather, B. E. "Assessment of Men: A Validity Study." M.S. thesis, Massachusetts Institute of Technology, 1964.

Meyer, H. H. "Assessment Centers at General Electric." Paper presented at a meeting of Development Dimensions, San Francisco, 1972.

Moses, Joseph L. "Assessment Center Performance and Management Progress." *Studies in Personnel Psychology*, Vol. 4 (January 1972), pp. 7-12.

Thomson, Harvey A. "Comparison of Predictor and Criterion Judgments of Managerial Performance Using the Multitrait-Multimethod Approach." *Journal of Applied Psychology*, Vol. 54 (December 1970), pp. 496-502. (Standard Oil Company.)

Wollowick, Herbert B., and McNamara, W. J. "Relationship of the Components of an Assessment Center to Management Success." *Journal of Applied Psychology*, Vol. 53 (October 1969), pp. 348-52. (IBM Corporation.)

TABLE I-1

Assessment Judgments and Field-Performance Ratings

Assessment Judgment	No. Men	No. Meeting Review Standards	Percentage Meeting Review Standards
More Than Acceptable	9	9	100%
Acceptable	32	19	60%
Less Than Acceptable	16	7	44%
Unacceptable	21	2	10%
Total	78	37	47%

Source: Douglas W. Bray and Richard J. Campbell, "Selection of Salesmen by Means of an Assessment Center," *Journal of Applied Psychology*, Vol. 52 (February 1968), p. 38. Copyright 1968 by the American Psychological Association. Reprinted by permission.

Note: $x^2 = 24.19$; $p < .001$.

FIGURE I-1

Percentage of Men in Each Group Who Were
"Above Average" in Performance at the First Level of Management

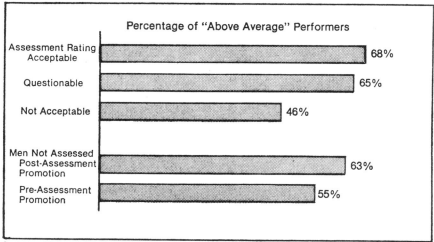

Source: Richard J. Campbell and Douglas W. Bray, "Assessment Centers: An Aid in
Management Selection," *Personnel Administration,* Vol. 30 (March–April 1967), p.
10. Reprinted by permission of the International Personnel Management Association,
1850 K St., N.W., Suite 870, Washington, D.C. 20006.

FIGURE I-2

Percentage of High Potential Men in Each Group

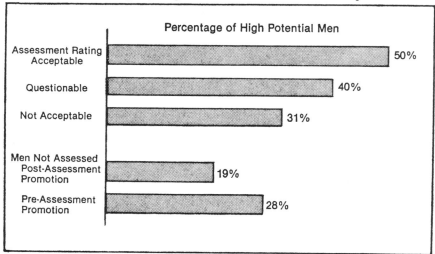

Source: Richard J. Campbell and Douglas W. Bray, "Assessment Centers: An Aid in
Management Selection," *Personnel Administration,* Vol. 30 (March–April 1967), p.
12. Reprinted by permission of the International Personnel Management Association,
1850 K St., N.W., Suite 870, Washington, D.C. 20006.

APPENDIX J

Honeywell Selection System
Performance Standards Statements
First-Line Factory Supervisors

I. Ability to plan for the accomplishment of goals. Includes determination of subgoals to support company goals, anticipating possible problems, gathering relevant information, setting of priorities, and implementing of plans.

Adjusts to changing conditions and reacts accordingly; accomplishes his planned results. A13

Is able to determine and set priorities despite interruptions from a variety of departments. A1

Foresees possible problems and has contingency plans ready. A23

Plans ahead, but remains flexible. A19

Can differentiate a short-term situation from a long-term situation. A6

Requisitions more or surpluses personnel when the work load changes. A5

Good on short-range planning, but makes no long-range plans. A14

Tends to overcommit himself. A22

Makes plans before weighing all the facts. A11

Plans do not take into account changes in the product mix. A9

Is reluctant to delegate work which could be done by someone else. A3

Is not adequately aware of company goals—both short- and long-range—when he makes his plans. A8

Gets involved doing the work, rather than supervising it. A4

Makes plans, but they are unrelated to company goals. A15

Has difficulty meeting deadlines and hates to commit himself. A2

Occasionally spends a day or more on small problems (e.g., tracking down a $1.80 charge on his budget printout). A21

Considers planning alone sufficient, without action to implement it. A18

Makes sure he always has enough work on hand, even if it means missing a schedule date. A7

Plans come apart under pressure. A12

His plans are usually grandiose and unjustifiable. A10

Makes no plans, but reacts to the latest or loudest demands. A16

Planning is incomplete and half-baked, many changes of direction. A17

Every change is a crisis or disaster. A20

II. Ability to administer rules and policies fairly and consistently. Includes knowledge of company rules and policies, and ability to interpret and explain the purpose of policies.

Has an awareness of established policies and procedures and insures that interpretation is consistent with company goals and precedents. B1

Sets an example when it comes to following policies and procedures. B9

Strives to understand and explain to his subordinates the intent of and reasoning behind the rules. B10

Takes and initiates prompt corrective action whenever the need becomes apparent. B7

Enforces all policies and procedures consistently whether he personally agrees with them or not. B6

Usually administers the policies to the letter, doesn't "waste" time on reasons for this. B4

Uses policies and procedures to the limit of the law, so he doesn't have to make any supervisory judgments. B5

Has an awareness of established policies and procedures, but tends to interpret things on his own. B2

Does not get an opinion from the area of authority before making a decision that might create a bad precedent. B3

Depends on others to interpret policies without checking unilaterally. B15

Usually administers policies and procedures fairly and consistently, but tends to show favoritism to certain employees. B8

Does not follow up to see if new policies and rules are being carried out. B12

Enforces all policies and procedures he agrees with, ignores the rest. B11

Depends on others to take actions which may be disagreeable or controversial. B14

Is not as familiar with policies and procedures as he should be and therefore does not administer them correctly. B17

Does not have an awareness of policies and procedures and makes no effort to become familiar with them. B16

Does not enforce policies and procedures. B13

Ignores infractions. B18

III. **Interdepartmental relations. Includes ability to develop and maintain good relations with other departments for the good of the company.**

Seeks ways to solve interdepartmental problems instead of looking for a department to blame for problems. C4

Responds rapidly to requests from other supervisors. C1

Confers regularly with other supervisors to keep the work flow smooth. C3

Maintains good relationships with other foremen and helps them whenever he can. C6

Is familiar with the operations of other departments so he knows who he could contact for assistance. C2

Has good "give and take" showing flexibility in working with other areas. C7

Recommends his best people to fill a job opening in another department. C5

Can deal effectively with janitors, maintenance men, and the service personnel even though they are off base. C13

Does not get engineering involved when necessary to help him solve his problems. C10

Bypasses lines of authority in dealing with other departments. C24

Is generally cooperative if it doesn't cost too much. C16

Is timid or hesitant to communicate with other areas. C8

Does not get all the facts before talking to other foremen about problems. C9

Shows lack of patience in getting a response from other departments. C15

Makes plans without regard to the effects the plans will have on other departments. C19

Gives preferential treatment to the departments his friends are in. C20

Overdefends his own employees when criticized by other supervisors. C26

Cannot discuss interdepartmental problems intelligently without tending to protect himself. C18

Habitually overstates his needs when requesting help from other departments. C22

Cooperates outwardly, but plays it in his favor. C14

Handles requests from other departments if and when he gets around to them. C21

Uses people on loan for the most undesirable jobs. C29

Is only interested in his own department and his own problems. C17

Will always accept people, but not loan them when another department is in dire need. C28

Never has time to help, but is always asking for it. C12

Creates unnecessary pressure on other departments for his own good. C25

Has a tendency to transfer undesirable employees rather than face the situation and take necessary action in his own area. C27

Rarely helps other departments. C11

Has no empathy for other supervisors or departments. C23

IV. **Ability to train and develop subordinates. Includes proper orientation of subordinates to company, department and job, motivation of subordinates, performance counselling, and other developmental methods such as rotation of job assignments.**

Has superior ability in selecting suitable men and training them to assume specific responsibilities. D8

Works closely with his subordinates teaching and coaching them to help them do a better job. D4

Establishes performance standards and objectives with each employee. D10

Maintains an excellent training program and atmosphere in department. D7

Tries to help each employee relate his job to the overall company operations and goals. D11

Is willing to recommend his best employees for promotional opportunities. D20

Keeps his employees informed of their job status—what their strong and weak points are and what they can do to correct their weaknesses. D17

Gives the employees the latitude they need to do their jobs effectively and to grow in their jobs. D12

Takes whatever action is necessary with below standard performers. D3

Informs employees of training and educational opportunities. D13

Listens to employees' recommendations for improvements and makes changes accordingly or explains reasons change cannot be made. D2

Is aware of obstacles facing employees and removes as many as possible. D18

Gives employees training that pertains to their work; avoids training that has no real potential benefit for the employee. D6

Sometimes delegates training to others, but does not retain the basic and overall responsibility for proper training. D19

Does not explain why the functions must be carried out in a certain manner. D26

Goes to or sends substitutes to every seminar and shows that he hears about whether relevant or not. D25

Does not pass on to subordinates the objectives of management and how this relates to how the subordinate does his job. D14

Trains people for job opportunities that are not likely to be realized. D23

Believes that his own position is strengthened by keeping his employees strictly in line and attending only to their immediate tasks. D21

Gives minimum effort to train or is motivated to do so only when compelled to by order or circumstance. D9

Is afraid to give his employees too much information about operations. D27

Feels that business pressures do not permit time to train. D5

Does not seek out good men and train them for future jobs, maybe even his own. D24

Will not upset good employee performance on a job by training or allowing the employee to seek a higher level of which he is capable. D16

Tends to forget about training because he is too busy. D15

Provides no training and discourages subordinates from participating in training programs. D22

Ignores training completely. D1

V. Initiative. Includes ability to seek out solutions, make decisions, take action, and meet deadlines.

Has drive to get things done, get work started, and keep it moving along to a satisfactory completion. E9

Makes things happen; does not wait for things to happen. E12

Recognizes situations needing attention and takes action up to his limit of authority. E18

Is a self-starter; rarely needs urging to complete tasks. E11

Takes time to deal with problems while they are "hot." E2

Does a good job of gathering and assessing the facts and making a decision on that basis. E13

Makes allowances in a busy schedule for contemplation of important decisions. E4

Normally tries to anticipate possible problems so there aren't many surprises or crises. E17

Calls for help or consultation if a problem is beyond his ability. E26

Takes action even though a problem is not his and he could ignore it and not get in trouble. E19

Shows great spurts of initiative and action, but is not consistent. E6

Frequently takes action based on the immediate need, without studying the total potential results of the action. E14.

Starts by himself, but stops at the first problem or interference. E10

Is reluctant to make decisions which have merit, but which may appear radical. E24

Reacts when problems are brought to his attention, but fails to seek out problems on his own. E22

Loses enthusiasm for a project once it has been approved. E25

Does not use all the resources at his disposal to help him get desired results. E21

Has many excuses for not obtaining results because of things which he feels are beyond his control. E16

Knows of situation needing attention, but takes no action until forced to do so. E23

Does only what is necessary to get by. E7

Has little initiative because of a fear of being wrong or making an error. (Lacks courage.) E5

Accepts things as they are because they have always been that way. E20

Is unable to make a decision under pressure; vacillates until the situation resolves itself or someone else takes it over. E15

Believes that the boss's job is to tell him what needs doing, and responds only to his boss's direction. E8

Must be urged and pressed to complete work. E3

Attempts to "pass the buck" rather than make his own decisions. E1

VI. Member of management. Ability to consider himself, express himself, and work as part of management. Includes knowing what is expected and disseminating company policy despite personal feelings.

Obtains as many relevant facts as possible, so management decisions can be based on sound reasoning instead of opinions. F1

Makes it a point to clarify objectives with management. F2

Fields his management position; he is a part of management rather than saying management made that rule. F12

Accepts management directives objectively and conveys this attitude to employer. F13

Is fair toward employees and still represents management in the eyes of the employer. F11

Tries to understand the intent of policies so as to interpret them for situations that are not black and white. F14

Makes recommendations to management to correct faulty policies or procedures, rather than complain about problems. F19

Makes constructive suggestions to management when an employee problem exists. F23

Keeps management informed of situations that could affect operations. F21

Gets a clarification of questionable policies prior to expressing himself. F9

Is willing to accept a cost increase, extra effort, etc., if it will result in net improvement in the total operations. F4

Does a good job of clearly expressing objections to policies to the proper departments or individuals. F3

Tries to understand how his operations affect other departments so the net result can be most effective. F8

Provides feedback to management with questions or comments if a policy seems unrealistic. F18

Gives company policies his personal endorsement and backing even if he does not completely agree with them. F7

Is willing to question a policy or procedure. F17

Informs management when he is being overloaded and cannot fulfill his responsibilities. F20

Unquestioningly applies rules to the letter, even in situations where this might be contrary to the intent. F22

Tends to identify with the employee against management, in order to cajole the employee into performing. F15

Is passive in his attitude toward company policies. F10

Blames "management" when he has to take controversial or disagreeable action. F16

Tends to be a loner; sets his own policies and priorities. F6

Sees all changes as threatening. F5

VII. Technical competence. Includes familiarity with technology, principles and processes of area supervised, and ability to suggest and effect improvements in the quality and quantity of work supervised.

Blends technical know-how and supervisory know-how very well. G12

Continually looks for ways of improving the organization methods of his department and the efficiency of his operations. G5

Is able to analyze and solve problems effectively. G15

Is conscious of customer's needs and, therefore, keeps a close watch on quality. G7

Is highly regarded and consulted by other supervisors. G3

Keeps up-to-date on the latest technological developments. G21

Questions engineering decisions and recommendations for greater understanding. G4

Understands related functions that affect his area. G11

Takes classes on his own time to improve technical competence because it will help do a better job. G13

Investigates and analyzes improved processes. G22

Has a working knowledge of all equipment and procedures performed in his department. G9

Allocates sufficient time to know what's happening, technically, in his department. G19

Knows enough to direct employees and help when needed. G16

Relies on support departments for technical work. G17

Has no technical background, but learns fast. G14

Has some background, but requires direction. G20

Concentrates on just certain aspects of his job in which he feels he is competent. G10

Knows he has reached his peak and is satisfied to remain in present position, therefore does not see how technical knowledge will benefit him. G6

Is overly competent technically—spends more time on technical duties than he does on supervisory duties. G25

Is reluctant to seek improvements on existing operations that seem to run "without problems." G18

Does not staff his area with the proper know-how. G8

Resists suggestions for process study or improvement because of potential implied criticism of his methods. G2

Pride causes him to *not* ask questions. G23

Has inadequate comprehension of job requirements. G24

Tries to ship below standard work, instead of solve the problem. G1

VIII. Human relations skills. Ability to get along well with others, communicate facts clearly and completely in a tactful manner, and get work done without adverse feelings.

Has ability to say or do what is best or is necessary, thoughtfully and with consideration; recognizes that there are two sides to most situations; therefore, chooses words carefully and acts considerately. H9

Is effective under difficult situations. H3

Feels a real concern for the other person, as an individual, whether he is subordinate or superior in rank. H8

Recognizes that employees have different backgrounds, desires, and goals and must be treated as individuals. H6

Is a good listener; communicates by listening, questioning, and discussing rather than just telling. H17

Gives an employee as much information as possible about company objectives and operations and what contribution he is making. H7

Shows enthusiasm for getting the job done, which rubs off on subordinates. H20

Can constructively criticize an employée's weakness without alienating the employee. H21

Greets each new employee as he comes under his supervision; provides proper orientation to work environment. H15

Disciplines in a constructive manner with a desire to change rather than punish. H11

Can deal effectively with all levels of management and support groups. H10

Double-checks to make sure an employee understands what's been said. H18

Has a sense of humor. H4

Recognizes that employees will reflect and sometimes amplify his attitude. H14

Contacts employees on a daily basis if even to say "good morning." H13

Lets a person blow off steam before he starts talking himself. H12

Tends to oversupervise and delegates responsibility, but with no authority. H2

Must make all decisions himself. H1

Creates a "persona non grata" climate for himself in other areas. H19

Is uncomfortable with subordinates; rarely communicates with them except when absolutely necessary. H5

Gets too familiar with his employees. H16

IX. Safety and housekeeping. Knows and enforces safe practices and procedures.

Immediately and consistently enforces safety rules; corrects unsafe conditions. I6

Generates an awareness and attitude toward safety with his subordinates. I9

Enforces wearing of protective devices where required. I7

Sells employees on the importance of safety for their sake. I16

Enforces all OSHA regulations and keeps abreast of all safety and housekeeping practices. I15

Exemplifies good safety and housekeeping traits. I10

Sets a good example. I8

Accepts responsibility for the appearance of his department and does not depend on maintenance to keep this in line. I5

Keeps up-to-date on safety rules, regulations, and how they apply. I13

Understands the need and rationale for safety and housekeeping. I11

Searches out safety violations. I14

Establises a safety group in his department. I12

Is a "nut" on housekeeping and safety. I3

Does enough to "get by." I4

Posts signs and reminders, but doesn't demonstrate personal concern. I20

Has to be continually reminded on housekeeping. I24

Blames poor housekeeping in his unit on other people. I1

Does not make his employees keep things in order. I2

Blames unfavorable safety rules on safety committee or OSHA rather than support the rules. I17

Makes exceptions to safety rules. I23

Feels that safety is the responsibility of the safety director. I22

Does not bring up or take action on established rules. I25

Does not insist that equipment be properly guarded. I26

Knows few safety rules and could care less. I21

Ignores all good safety and housekeeping rules. I18

Disregards safety rules. I19

X. Communications. Includes providing feedback to his superiors on status of projects, proper preparation, timely submission of required reports, and prompt and complete problem reporting.

Informs his supervisor of important matters; does not bore him with unnecessary information. J1

Communicates with employees on actions to be taken, explaining reasons; includes reasons for policies, practices, procedures, unusual circumstances. J12

Develops, with his boss, reports for the major factors by which departmental performance can be measured; provides these routinely. J11

Discusses major problems with supervisors; offers his solutions for critique. J7

Prepares reports which are clear, concise, and complete. J4

Communicates with employees on a daily basis by words and actions. J5

Fills supervisor in on problems and potential problems. J9

Puts problems in proper perspective. J6

Provides feedback on status of problems without being asked. J10

When he makes a decision, informs all persons who may be affected. J14

Offers recommendations and alternatives for each problem situation reported. J13

Is capable of selling his ideas orally and in writing. J3

Explains standards that have been established for the department. J8

Keeps minor personnel problems to himself. J2

Does not use simple terms; may be trying to impress others with his vocabulary. J16

Asks his boss for too much information. J18

Only provides information when questioned about specific items. J15

Does not communicate to his subordinates all pertinent information. J27

Tells his supervisor only those things which make him appear favorable. J24

Does not submit paperwork on time; i.e., change notices, reviews, leaves, terminations, etc. J28

Is continually late on information required for regular reports. J19

Does not let people know where they stand. J20

Insufficient communications with superior or subordinates. J17

Provides feedback only when favorable. J26

Gives an order without any explanation. J23

Fails to provide the facts necessary to make a decision. J22

Has not been a good listener, cuts off or interrupts constantly, or even argues. This discourages communications. J21

Does not make it easy for an employee to approach him. J29

Does not follow up on promises to employees. J25

XI. Willingness to accept responsibility. Includes attending to assigned duties, following up on details, and meeting commitments.

Is not afraid of responsibility and of being blamed for failure. K14

Implements corrective action to prevent recurrence of a given problem. K4

If there is uncertainty regarding whose responsibility a job is, will discuss it with all concerned to resolve the question. K6

Makes decisions based on facts rather than wait for backup. K10

Accepts responsibility for mistakes for all members of the department. K8

Defends unfavorable or unpopular decisions on part of management rather than blaming it on "them." K5

Is willing to delegate responsibility when the situation warrants it— without abdication. K18

Is willing to spend his own time on self-development. K12

Volunteers to work on special projects. K17

Maintains an effective bring-up system. K13

Assumes more responsibility than he should. K3

Ignores a need unless it is clearly assigned to him. K11

Is unwilling to make decisions which would hurt someone's feelings. K19

Does not speak up until decision is made or completed. K7

Is unwilling to put in additional hours as necessary to meet deadlines. K9

Has reasons why things are the way they are instead of how he can correct situation. K1

Generates defensive paperwork. K16

Fails to insure the successful completion of projects by failure to follow up and take action. K21

Tends to blame others for mistakes in his department. K20

Avoids his position's responsibilities and wants someone else to make decisions to avoid criticism. K15

Is a master at passing the buck; takes others awhile to realize the buck has been passed. K2

XII. Integrity, trustworthiness, and honesty.

Is completely trustworthy. L19

Is very honest and tells it like it is regardless of the consequences. L16

Manages by example, and people follow the lead. L22

All of his employees respect him because his performance appraisals are honest and fair. L18

Assumes responsibility for the company property in his department and for the condition and care of equipment, tools, material, and supplies used in his department. L24

Has the courage of his convictions and habits. L21

Does not take advantage of his position. L17

Does not downgrade his boss to subordinates or anyone else. L23

Attempts to scuttle rumors rather than add to them. L20

Is honest about most things that he considers important. L2

Will answer a question truthfully, but won't volunteer any damaging or unpleasant information. L11

Never lies, but occasionally purposely withholds facts. L14

Tells boss what he thinks the boss wants to hear. L4

Normally tries to rationalize or shift the blame for any apparent problem. L13

Makes personal use of company materials and equipment because his position justifies it. L10

Nearly always exaggerates. L1

Tells half the story, puts emphasis on wrong part. L15

Tries to work things to his best advantage rather than for the good of the company. L8

Allows false rumors to circulate rather than trying to stop them when he knows better. L5

Bends policies, practices, and procedures for his own or his employees' benefit. L6

Covers up deficiencies because he doesn't want to accept the responsibility of correcting them. L7

Will do whatever is necessary to maintain his own position. L12

Will deceive anyone if he thinks the end result justifies it. L3

Disseminates company confidential information. L9

XIII. Department administration. Forecasting, budgeting, cost control, cost improvement, recordkeeping, report preparation, inventory control, and justification of capital expenditures.

Directs his efforts towards the company's cost performance goals. M7

Is able to cope with changes of budget; adjusts department operations as necessary. M4

Controls costs and keeps budget even under severe circumstances. M14

Very honest with most problems or budgets—gets everything out in the open. M5

Keeps a close eye on factors influencing cost and how they affect his budget. M13

Recognizes when budget guidelines should be overridden for logical and profitable reasons. M9

Keeps good data on overall operation of his department. M10

Has his people or clerks keep information in front of him so he can make good decisions. M2

Reports to his superior if there are inefficiencies or mistakes in the organizational setup. M6

Delegates to others recordkeeping and clerical functions that can be done by others. M12

Wants cost improvement on jobs, even though they are trouble free and add more indirect labor. M1

Handles capital expenditures and any other spending very well, but falls down on controlling costs and good planning for efficient operation. M21

Operates by the budget despite changed economic conditions and/or changed company objectives. M20

Concentrates on day-to-day problems; fails to look past the end of his nose. M11

Does not keep track of work in process in his department. M8

Justifies variances based on opinion rather than facts. M3

Does not keep good control of paperwork. M18

Has difficulty relating costs, forecasting, etc., to actual situations. M17

Does a minimum job on records, forecasting, etc. M19

Continues to do things the way we've always done them, without making an analysis to see if improvement could be made. M15

Pads the expense budget to make sure he'll be in good shape next year. M16

Index

industry nature,
  influence on selection practices, 43-
  46. *See also* institutional factors
initiative,
  influence on selection, 67, 69
institutional factors,
  defined, 13
  influence on selection practices, 43-
  56, 76, 79
"interest profile," 147-50. *See also*
  selection-by-testing program
internal labor market,
  defined, 13
International Business Machines, 93,
  103, 121

job history,
  influence on selection, 63-64, 77
job knowledge,
  influence on selection, 67, 69
Jones, W. S., 90n

Kirkpatrick, James J., 87n
Kraut, Allen I., 113n, 114n, 115n,
  116n, 117n

labor demand,
  influence on selection practices, 33-
  35. *See also* environmental factors
Lawshe, C. H., 4n
leaderless group discussion, 99
leadership,
  influence on selection, 67-68, 69
line managers,
  as assessors, 95, 103-6
location,
  influence on selection practices, 36-
  40. *See also* environmental factors
Lopez, Felix M., 90n
Lupton, Daniel E., 116n, 117n

"machine tender," 29n
MacKinnon, Donald W., 96n, 106n
McNamara, Walter J., 103n
McQuitty, Louis L., 18
McReynolds, Paul, 111n
Maloney, J. C., 4n
management,
  and selection, 49
Management Progress Study, 93, 95,
  110
Mandell, Milton M., 5n
marital status,
  influence on selection, 65-66
market orientation,
  influence on selection practices, 46.
  See also institutional factors
Mechanical Comprehension Test, 145

method of critical incident, 128
Michigan Bell, 93-122 passim, 155.
  See also assessment center method; Personnel Assessment Program
military service,
  influence on selection, 65-66
minorities, 161-69 passim
  and formal selection practices, 93,
  94, 118, 121, 142-44
  and informal selection practices, 35-
  36, 37-39, 40-43, 44, 65
mobility,
  defined, 13
Molander, Chris, 5n
Moses, Joseph L., 91n, 92n, 93n, 100n
Mussen, Paul H., 91n

"narrow band" selection technique,
  155
National Labor Relations Act, 8
National Labor Relations Board, 8n
Naylor, James C., 137n
"new work force," 11
New York City, 9
nonferrous smelter, 12-80 passim
  selection practices, 19, 20
Northrup, Herbert R., 8n, 32n, 35n,
  42n

objective performance numbers, 124-
  25. *See also* criteria; "performance standards"
objectivity,
  of tests, 88
Occupational Safety and Health Act
  of 1970, 10-11
O'Connor, Edward J., 169n
Office of Federal Contract Compliance
  Programs, 10, 167
  guidelines, 163
Office of Management and the Budget,
  106
organizational analysis, 16-17, 77, 79-
  80
organization memberships,
  influence on selection, 62-63
Overall Assessment Rating. *See*
  assessment center method
Owens, W. A., 146

paper-and-pencil test, 99, 104, 123-57
  passim, 163
paper manufacturer, 12-80 passim
  selection practices, 19, 20
Patten, Thomas H., Jr., 7n
Peace Corps, 102-3
Penney, J. C., 102

Racial Policies of American Industry Series

Order from: Kraus Reprint Co., Route 100, Millwood, New York 10546